H U M O R
The Magic of Genie

Other Book Coauthored by Jeanne Robertson
How The Platform Professionals "KEEP 'EM LAUGHIN'"

H U M O R
The Magic of Genie

by
Jeanne Robertson

Rich Publishing Co.
10611 CREEKTREE • HOUSTON, TEXAS 77070

To Jerry,
who loves me even when I
do not keep my sense of humor.

First Edition 1990
First Printing, January 1990
Second Printing, July 1990
Third Printing, September 1991
Fourth Printing, September 1993
Fifth Printing, September 1995
Sixth Printing, September 1998

Library of Congress Catalog Card No. 89-62130
ISBN 0-9607256-9-5

Printed in the United States of America

CONTENTS

With a 16 Page Picture Center Section

PREFACE   **VII**

PART I   **1**

About the Author—Jeanne Robertson   3

PART II   **7**

Characteristics of a Sense of Humor   9
Prerequisites for Developing a Sense of Humor   13

PART III   **15**

Potion 1: Laugh at Yourself   17
Potion 2: Look for the Humor in Everyday
          Situations   45
Potion 3: Create Your Own Humor   73
Potion 4: Associate with People Who Have a
          Sense of Humor   101
Potion 5: Influence Others to Develop a Sense of
          Humor   131
Potion 6: See the Humor in Stressful, Awkward,
          or Unpleasant Situations   157
Potion 7: Take Humor Breaks/Collect Humor Cues   185

PREFACE

Much has been written in recent years concerning the benefits of laughter and having a sense of humor. The research of Norm Cousins in his best seller *The Anatomy of an Illness* supported the thesis that laughter has healing powers. Others have presented empirical evidence to support the noteworthy conclusions of Cousins. Numerous researchers have indicated that a sense of humor is one of the most significant characteristics of executives or people in leadership roles, while other writers have espoused the power of a sense of humor in enhancing a person's mental well-being and social status. Few people would debate the claims of these writers who suggest that a good sense of humor is one of the most important characteristics a person can possess.

Since the benefits of humor have been well-documented and are widely accepted, this book focuses attention on how to develop a sense of humor. Seven magical potions are offered to help you make humor a significant aspect of your life. It is my ardent wish that this book will not only enhance your sense of humor and be beneficial to you and those who share your life, but will also provide you with hours of laughter through the stories and personal experiences which I have selected to illustrate the steps for developing a sense of humor.

The seven potions or steps in developing a sense of humor presented in this book were developed over a twenty-five year period both from my experiences as a professional humorous speaker and as a student of humor. As a guide to enable the reader to better understand and appreciate the essence of my personal beliefs regarding a sense of humor, outlined below are the most important tenets of my humor philosophy.

1. I believe a sense of humor is one of the most important assets a person can possess. Although I am intrigued by all the new research on the value and importance of laughter for health reasons, I think the real value in humor is that it enables us to enjoy every day and our particular life situations. It also enables the people around us to enjoy their days a little more.

2. I do not think that being funny necessarily means a person has a sense of humor. We all know funny people who are not so congenial when a problem arises. I agree with Steve Allen that developing a sense of humor is: "THE CREATING OF A LIFESTYLE IN WHICH HUMOR IS A CONSCIOUS AND SIGNIFICANT ELEMENT." A sense of humor is simply a lifestyle.

3. I do believe that a "good" sense of humor can be developed and enhanced, and that this is not a time-consuming process.

Desire, determination, and a little direction are the only prerequisites for improving your humor aptitude.

4. I believe that through our actions we can influence the people around us to develop or keep a sense of humor. When we work to influence others to do this, we continue to develop our own sense of humor.

PART I

ABOUT THE AUTHOR—
JEANNE ROBERTSON

The Beginning

In 1956, I could have written the following letter:

Dear Abby,

I am a 13-year-old girl in the seventh grade. I live in a little southern town called Graham, North Carolina, and I have been told that I have a thick, southern accent. Abby, I weigh 160 pounds . . . and I wear a size 11B shoe.

And there is one more thing. Already, at age 13—barefooted with my hair MASHED DOWN—I am six feet, two inches tall.

Tell me, pleeeease, Abby, what are my chances of ever being in the Miss America Pageant?

—High Pockets

The reply would have probably read:

Dear High,

Forget the Miss America Pageant, and develop a sense of humor.

—Abby

And Years Later

Years have passed since that letter could have been written. Today, I am a woman who, believe me, is a LOOONG WAY from even remembering the seventh grade.

My southern accent has gotten a lot mo'ah su'thurn.

I still weigh in at one hundred and sixty pounds. Maintaining this weight has been a struggle, and it is an accomplishment. But don't be too impressed; it has had a slight downward shift over the course of time. I just hope it never shifts all the way to my feet. I still wear size 11B shoes.

I am still six feet, two inches tall.

But I am also a woman who has the honor of being THE TALLEST CONTESTANT TO HAVE EVER COMPETED IN THE MISS AMERICA PAGEANT FROM ANY STATE IN THE UNION AT ANY TIME. Don't be overly impressed with this either. This also makes me, "The tallest contestant to ever LOSE in the Miss America Pageant."

I did win the title of Miss Congeniality, however, and I guess there are those who might be impressed by the Miss Congeniality title. Those who know better, realize . . . Miss Congeniality is usually the contestant whom the others believe to be LEAST LIKELY to win the title of Miss America.

Pageant Talk

Now, years later, when I give speeches in my home state of North Carolina, I often ask my audiences if anyone remembers seeing me perform my talent on television at the Miss America

Pageant. A smattering of hands always go up. This fascinates me . . . because I never got to perform my talent on television at the Miss America Pageant! And this was probably just as well. My talent was playing the ukulele.

"Sure," you may be thinking, "but if you got all the way to the Miss America Pageant, you must have really been able to play that ukulele." Wrong! I knew four chords. As I played those four chords, I was singing the best I could sing. So I listed my talent as "singing and accompanying myself on the ukulele." Most newspeople reported it as "comedy," and even I realized that I probably was not going to score high in the talent department with a ukulele and four chords, to say nothing of my lack of singing ability.

I know also for a fact that playing the ukulele is not the worst talent that has ever been presented in a pageant. At a local pageant I emceed, there was one PITIFUL girl who PLAYED THE COMB for her talent. (We are talking Pit-i-ful.) This contestant really wanted to win. She had her high school shop class make a BIG COMB. They wheeled that big comb out on stage on a little comb cart, and she picked it up and went to town! I stood on the side of the stage and wished she had been at the Miss America Pageant when I was there. Then I could have been assured of at least finishing 49th out of 50 girls.

She was not THAT good! But she knew something very important. Something I had learned when I was 6′2″ at age 13, and something we all can learn and benefit from: **she had learned the importance of a sense of humor.** On this particular night, she used her humor to work the audience; and when she finished with that comb routine, everybody was on their feet.

. . . which is what usually happens when someone plays the National Anthem in the talent competition.

The Magic of Humor

HOW could this happen? How could a 6′2″, 160 lb. young woman from a small southern town wind up in the Miss America

Pageant? Playing the ukulele? It could have happened because somewhere along the way, this Jeanne (or Genie, for all magical purposes) learned the magic of a sense of humor.

Humor served me well as a child and as Miss North Carolina. It carried me through competing in the Miss America Pageant, teaching and coaching basketball for nine years, and bringing up a 6'8" son named Beaver. It continues to work for me now. Today, I am a professional speaker classified as a humorist. Over 130 times a year, I speak to audiences all over the United States, as well as Mexico, Canada and other foreign countries—including California. While balancing a career as a professional speaker with being a wife and mother, a sense of humor has been an important magical thread that has pulled many things together in my life, and greatly increased the joy of living.

After twenty-five years of traveling as a humorous speaker, and observing people in all types of interesting situations, I often ask myself and others, "Why don't more people have a good sense of humor? Why do those who sometimes exhibit a sense of humor often lose it? Why don't people work to develop their senses of humor?" I get a zillion answers to my questions such as, "I don't know how to be funny . . . don't know any jokes or one liners to use . . . I would like to be humorous, but no one laughs at my stories."

The responses to my questions indicate that people perceive a sense of humor in different ways. Therefore, to lead or stimulate your thinking about developing humor, it is necessary to clearly describe my beliefs about both the characteristics of a sense of humor and the prerequisites for developing a sense of humor. This will, I believe, open the door for a better understanding and allow you to grasp and apply "The Magic of Genie" in developing a personal approach.

PART II

CHARACTERISTICS OF A
SENSE OF HUMOR

Think about what is generally meant by having a good sense
of humor. In the United States we have become very attuned to stand-up comedy, often off-color and laced with four-
letter words. We have become so attuned, in fact, that when we
hear the words "sense of humor" we often think of someone with
microphone in hand, making the masses laugh. And why not?
Turn on the television any night of the week, flip the channels
long enough, and you will find a stand-up comedian in the
middle of a routine or a sitcom in full swing.

Comedy has become such a part of our lives that great-
grandmothers down to junior high students recognize one liners,
ad-libs, and "good timing," and they can analyze ten-minute
routines like professional entertainment critics. (Of course, most
great-grandmothers also say that they remember when "good

timing" was having children when they wanted to.) Indeed, comedy surrounds us so much that when we hear a comment such as, "We need to keep a sense of humor in business," or "It is important to keep a sense of humor when dealing with teenagers," many think someone is referring to telling funny stories and coming up with quick, hilarious remarks. For many, having a sense of humor in a day-to-day working relationship means patting business associates on the back and laughing . . . when what they said was not even funny, or always being able to tell the latest joke that was on television the previous night. Often people think that having a sense of humor means always being ready with the witty comeback or being able to keep the luncheon group in hysterics. This certainly has its place. We all enjoy being around funny people, and thank goodness, from my perspective as a humorist, that people also enjoy listening to speakers who make them laugh while illustrating serious points. But is "being funny" the same as having a sense of humor? No. Everyone knows very funny people who do not have a good sense of humor.

All too often this type of individual—the funny person—experiences frequent highs and lows. One day he is on top of the world, sky high with enthusiasm, everybody's funny friend, and the supposedly perfect, funny parent. Everything is going fine and on schedule. There are no crises, no last minute forms to fill out, and no breakdown in the car pool. But the next day or even the next hour when there is a problem, he is just as likely to sink to a low or react with anger, and the people who work and live with this individual on a day-to-day basis figure it out in a hurry. They never know if the sense of humor is on or off, so the best thing is to stick a toe in the water with each encounter and see what the temperature will be on that occasion.

No, being funny does not necessarily mean a person has a sense of humor. Rather than just possessing the ability to make other people laugh, a sense of humor is more a lifestyle in which humor is a significant and conscious element. If you agree with that statement, then the question becomes how to create that lifestyle: how to make humor a conscious and significant element in your everyday life. In other words, how do you develop a sense of humor?

At this point I must remind you that everyone has a sense of humor. I repeat: EVERYONE has a sense of humor. It is just that some people have such a baaaad one that it does not help them in any way. Unfortunately, they never realize a poor sense of humor may very well hurt their professional careers as well as their private lives. In this book, when I refer to a sense of humor, I am referring to the kind that helps you: the sense of humor that works to one's advantage—good humor that is a conscious and significant element in one's lifestyle.

PREREQUISITES
FOR DEVELOPING
A SENSE OF HUMOR

There are three prerequisites for developing or expanding a sense of humor. I call them the three "D's": DESIRE—DETERMINATION—DIRECTION.

Desire is, of course, the starting point for virtually all our achievements in life. In others words, to reach a goal or accomplish a project you really gotta wanna. A belief in the results of scientific studies which emphasize the value of possessing a good sense of humor and the positive effects a humorous attitude has on a person's health, happiness, and success in life, should be all that is needed to instill a strong desire to improve one's humor level. With desire firmly fixed you are well on your way to developing your sense of humor.

The second prerequisite for developing a sense of humor is determination. Determination is necessary to cope with any

13

modification in one's present lifestyle because change evolves with time and effort. While the concept of seven magical potions may cast an image of instant results like those attributed to most Genies, the development of habits is not instant. It takes both time and determination.

The maturing of humor is just like the magic done by the stage magician. There is a logical explanation as to why something happens, and as with the stage magician, practice makes perfect. Granted, it does take time to turn these steps into habits, but satisfaction is found in knowing that there do not have to be any earth-shattering changes in your life in order to meet your humor goal. You do not have to quit your job and try out for a comedy club. Nor do you have to become the wit of your social set. You merely become determined to change your lifestyle in keeping with the way you view the world as you absorb the potions to increase your humor awareness. Then before you know it, you will be reflecting a lifestyle in which humor is a conscious and significant element as you discover the Magic of Genie—a sense of humor.

If you have the desire to develop a sense of humor and are determined to do it, then all you need is the final "D"—direction. The primary purpose of this book is to offer this direction by presenting the steps that will enable you to develop a sense of humor. I call them "magic potions" because as they are put into practice, a certain magic does seem to take place. Each potion, when digested, influences a change in lifestyle with humor as a priority.

The balance of this book is devoted largely to the seven magic potions, each representing a simple step to achieve an ever expanding sense of humor. I suggest that you read or drink in each potion, one sip or one step at a time. Savor each magic elixir slowly. Let each potion become a powerful stimulant as it illustrates how you can possess a wonderful sense of humor. Enjoy the variety of my many anecdotes, antics and pratfalls. Then begin to put into practice each potion, and notice the change toward a happier, healthier, more positive lifestyle.

PART III

Potion 1
Laugh at Yourself

The consensus of all those who study humor, think about it, write or deliver it, is that the most important ingredient in developing a sense of humor is being able to laugh at yourself. I wholeheartedly concur that to build a sense of humor it is essential that we do just that: LAUGH AT OURSELVES. Easily said, but how is it accomplished? How do individuals who readily admit they do not laugh at themselves capture the magic of doing so?

There are three ingredients that go into the magic potion of laughing at yourself:

- Accepting the things about yourself that cannot be changed.
- Identifying and accepting your unique characteristics.
- Sharing your bloopers, blunders, and put-downs with others.

ACCEPTING THE UNCHANGEABLE

We can never truly learn to laugh at ourselves until we learn to accept the things about ourselves that cannot be changed. Most of us have a wish list of things we would change about our physical make-up if it were possible. There are some things that could be changed through surgery or with the power of paints and powder. But, for the most part, we must learn to accept those things that are either impossible or impractical to change. Here are some of the perplexities that I have faced and the results of learning to accept the unchangeable.

Exceeding the Norm

I can't explain why I am six feet, two inches tall. No one else in the family is. Daddy came close to six feet, but even that's not so tall for a man.

Mother was five feet, five inches tall. My sisters, Katherine and Andrea, are each approximately five feet, five inches. All the rest of the cousins, aunts, uncles, and grandparents cannot even classify as medium height. They are just plain short.

I was tall for any age from the day I was born. However, I really did not realize how tall I was until the day I entered the first grade. After looking around over the heads of my classmates, I realized that I was the tallest person in the room. Questions to Mom and Dad such as "Did you hold her back?" also gave me a hint that I was a little different. Accepting my unusual height during these early years would prove to be a real challenge.

Learning to Cope

Elementary school recess stands out as a time when I was definitely learning to laugh at myself. The teacher would say, "Go outside, children, and jump rope." Sure! Classmates held the ends of the rope and I stood nearby swaying my body forward and back getting ready to "run in." They tried with all their might to get the rope over my head, but every time it would come around and whop me right in the face!

One day I thought I was smart. I got two milk crates from the school cafeteria and had each rope turner stand on one. "Now get that rope over my head!" I shouted, and proceeded with my running in. They did as instructed. The rope arched up and swung over me, clearing my head by several inches. Then it curved down, connecting sharply with the back of my knees as it cut my feet out from under me!

I had it made when it came to the playground chinning bar, though. All of my buddies jumped and pulled, kicking their feet in the air as they struggled to reach the steel bar that loomed over their heads. I just waited. Timing was everything. At the appropriate moment, I'd walk up and put my chin flat on the bar—a tactic that always brought gales of laughter from my classmates. It was like magic. They laughed and laughed, and I loved it.

Perhaps it was at recess that I discovered that I enjoyed being the center of attention. Being different made me so. I was the only person in grade school who could jump rope in a squat position. It was fun to stand on my tiptoes with my chin resting on the chinning bar. It was also in elementary school that the saying began that is now famous among my friends when we are at large gatherings, "Let's all meet at Jeanne!"

Slam Jam

Then in the fifth grade, a great thing happened. One day the teachers gathered all the girls from both fifth grade classes in the gymnasium and taught us how to play basketball. (We learned everything in thirty minutes, a fact that amazed me later when I majored in physical education and coached basketball for nine years.) The day it was announced that our class was to play the other class in a Big Game, everyone said, "We're glad we've got Jeanne!" I beamed. Being tall was not so bad.

It was evident to anyone who saw me at the age of ten that I was a tall young lady. But there is tall and then there is T-A-L-L. My folks, teachers, and other adults thought I would stop growing about then, and many in my class would catch up with me. Wrong. I had just begun my spurt, and when the smoke cleared at thirteen, I was six feet, two inches tall, weighed 160 pounds, and wore a size 11B shoe.

One day when I was in the middle of this growth spurt, I came home from school and went straight to bed. I slept a lot during those years. Several hours later I awoke to a darkened room and my parents whispering in the hall. Mother peeped in, but I played possum and she closed the door.

"What's she doing?" my father asked.

Mom heaved a big sigh. "She's just lying there . . . growing."

Getting the Jump

My Aunt Willie in Tallassee, Alabama, was the most diplomatic of all my relatives, careful never to make any comment that might hurt someone's feelings. Maybe if you're a little girl growing up with a name like Willie, you develop greater sensitivity about things. But even Aunt Willie had to catch herself the first time she saw me after my big growth spurt. "My goodness," she gasped to Mother. "What a . . . healthy child!"

Knowing that we would get this reaction whenever we visited our Alabama relatives, my parents had the wisdom to make a game out of it, rather than ignoring it or quickly changing the subject. As we approached their hometowns, Auburn and Luverne, we each guessed about how many times I'd hear, "My, how you've grown!" within a certain time limit. It was a contest. It was fun.

Because of the game, instead of shrinking back or having my feelings hurt, I eagerly awaited the phrase that was sure to come. When it did, I smiled and added it to the list. Sometimes in a room full of relatives, each commenting, "My, how you've grown," Mother, Daddy, Katherine, and I did not dare look at each other for fear of bursting out in laughter. We were working our own little magic, and the relatives didn't even know it.

On one trip, Daddy decided we had about enough of that particular game. He had another idea. When we arrived and everyone came running to the car, I jumped out and before they could say a word, shouted, "My, how I've grown!" The relatives stopped speechless in their tracks. And then they laughed.

Not only did my parents help me stockpile funny answers to routine questions about my height, they also came up with some pretty sharp answers of their own. Once I heard a woman say to mother, "It's difficult to believe you had a daughter that size."

"Oh," gushed Mother, "she wasn't that size when I had her. She was MUCH smaller."

Comebacks and Squelches

Over the years, I have noticed something about these comments. People feel compelled to walk up to perfect strangers and say, "You're tall" or "You're short." They rarely feel compelled to say to someone, "Gee, your eyes are a little too close together," or "When I was a child, I stepped on a bug about the size of that wart on your chin."

At age thirteen, I would be stumbling down the streets of Graham, trying to get my arms, my legs, AND my body going in the same direction at the same time. This was not automatic. I had to concentrate. All my friends walked along, casually drinking soft drinks and chatting, while I was thinking, "Left foot. Right foot."

Grownups I didn't know would come up to me on the street and shout, "LITTLE GIRL, CAN I ASK YOU SOMETHING?" (Shorter people think that taller people are all hard of hearing. They always shout at us.) I replied, "Yes, sir, but if you'll stop shouting, you will not attract such a large crowd."

The grownup would then ask, "How tall are you?" Imagine what a question like that from a perfect stranger does to a thirteen-year-old girl who is trying to move along inconspicuously. The first time it happened I felt funny inside. I got home . . . I don't know how . . . got in my room, stretched out across two beds, and I cried. In a day or so, when another stranger asked, "How tall are you?" I knew I was going to hear this one question the rest of my life, and I have.

When asked how long a person's legs should be, Abraham Lincoln supposedly said, "Long enough to reach the ground." I have had to come up with some humorous responses, too.

You're tall!

—Oh, no! I wasn't when I got up this morning! What am I going to do? None of my clothes are going to fit!

How tall are you, anyway?

—ANYWAY you look at it, I'm six feet, two inches tall.
—Tall enough, obviously.

Are you standing on something?

—My feet.

How did you get to be so tall?

—Pills.
—Spinach.
—Chocolate.

Did you get your father's height?

—No, this is all mine. He has his own height.

Were you born tall?

—Yes. My birthday is September 21st, 22nd, and 23rd.

Have you always been this tall?

—No, I was only 23 inches when I was born.

Where do you find your clothes?

—Usually in the closet. Sometimes under the bed.

How tall are you?

—I'm five feet, seven inches. I do all this with make-up.

There are dozens of curt comebacks and snappy squelches for curious questions. One tall person I met said, "The next time someone asks me 'How's the weather up there?' I'm going to tell him it's raining and spit on the top of his head!" However, I prefer responses that don't attack the asker, that leave them smiling and perhaps a little more aware of the humor of being human.

Food for Thought

Questions and comments about my height have continued into adulthood and have provided me with many opportunities to laugh. On one occasion I went into a grocery store where I do not normally shop. The clerk at the counter was much shorter than I, and as she began putting my food in the bag, she began to look at me. She gazed upward and if she caught my eye, quickly looked back down. I turned to look at a magazine, and when she thought I could not see her, she looked over the counter to see if I was standing on something. If I turned toward her, she snapped back and continued putting things in the bag. When she thought I was thoroughly engrossed in a story, she turned her head toward the next cash register and whispered loud enough to be heard in the produce department, "Myrtle! Get over here! You ain't gonna believe this!" Myrtle came bustling over.

"Go around the counter and check out them feet," encouraged the clerk in what she thought was a whisper.

Finally, the clerk could not stand it. She had to ask. "How tall are you, honey?"

I looked up from the magazine. "I am six feet, two inches tall."

"Ah, come on." She shook her head. "I don't believe that. I don't believe you're any six feet, two inches tall . . . and neither does Myrtle." Myrtle nodded in agreement.

"You're right," I answered. "I'm five-fourteen."

The woman drew herself up proudly. "I KNEW you weren't over no SIX FEET TALL!"

Correction Please

And, of course, there was the time I stood up to get off an airplane, and the man in the seat behind me looked up and blurted "Jesus Christ!" I turned, smiled, and said, "No . . . Jeanne Robertson."

Childish Candor

Not too long ago, I passed a little girl in a grocery store whom I guessed to be about five years old. As I walked down the aisle, I heard her exclaim to her mother, "She's tall-l-l!" Her mother did what most good mothers would do. She jerked her arm and said, "Shsss! She'll hear you."

The little girl was only five, but had enough sense to question, "Doesn't she know?"

I know.

A New Question

Several years ago, I finally reached a point where I thought that I had heard every possible question or comment about being tall. I was wrong. I was to emcee a beauty pageant in a little town in North Carolina not far from where I live. Because of the simplicity of the competition, I just needed to be on hand for a walk-through rehearsal the afternoon of the pageant. I played tennis that morning in my hometown until the last possible minute, and when I could wait no longer, I threw my evening gown in the back seat of my car and drove over to practice the contestants walking across the stage.

No one was at the auditorium when I arrived. They had all gone to a luncheon, but I knew they would be back shortly, so I just stood in my little tennis dress and waited.

Two men came in to sweep the auditorium and get ready for the pageant. They began to look at me funny. I am accustomed to this. When you are six feet, two inches tall, you get looked at "funny" every day of your life. Before long, though, they began to push their big brooms over toward where I was standing, and I knew it was just a matter of time until one of them asked the routine question, "How tall are you?"

This time, I decided I was going to come out ahead. I turned away from them and acted as though I did not know they were in the room, but you can tell when two people are standing right behind you, staring. Before they could say a word, I wheeled around and exclaimed, "I'm six feet, two inches tall!"

They jumped back. "We knew it! We KNEW you were six feet, two inches tall . . . but that ain't what we came over here to ask you."

I thought they were going to say, "Weren't you in the Miss America Pageant?" I stood up straight, held my stomach in (which made me dizzy), and said, "Go ahead, ask me whatever you want to."

One of them said, "We've got a five-dollar bet riding on this answer. We want to ask you one question and let you answer it, and one of us will be five dollars richer."

I thought to myself, "I've heard ALL the questions anyone can ask me about being tall," but I said, "O.K. I'm game. Go ahead. What's your question?"

One of them started shaking his index finger at me. "Now you tell the truth. Aren't you that big, six-foot-two tennis player what was a man, and now is a woman?"

I said, "I am a woman now. I have always been a woman, and I ALWAYS WILL BE a woman."

One of them hit the other one on the shoulder and said, "See, I told you. You can't always go by BIG LEGS."

Finding a Niche

When the song "Short People" was recorded in the seventies, it reminded me of a song called "Long Tall Sally" that was released just about the time I reached the finishing stages of growing long and tall. My classmates immediately nicknamed me after the song, and I could not decide whether I was hurt or loved the attention.

My Daddy said, "You can't prevent something like this from happening, Jeanne. Smile and try to enjoy it. At least everybody knows who you are." Then he added something that has turned out to be the basis for my philosophy of humor, something that I believe will work for everyone. He said, "You cannot change being tall, honey, but if you can accept it and learn to laugh at yourself, you're going to come out ahead."

Asset or Liability

Daddy was right. I didn't plan to be a professional speaker as a child. I wanted to be a prima ballerina. But it didn't take long to figure out that few ballet companies would be willing to pay four male dancers to hoist their female star up in the air. (Get her up on the count of seven!)

Oh, I studied dancing. Most little girls growing up in Graham, North Carolina, are exposed to dancin'. However, the handwriting was on the wall, when one day the instructor gave everyone a tutu and tossed me a "four-four."

An interesting fact is that as a young child, I would never have chosen to be six feet, two inches tall. I certainly would not have included unusual height on my list of desired physical characteristics. Yet, at an early age I took a good look at my unusual circumstances and accepted the fact that I was not going to get any shorter. I certainly could not go on a diet, lose three inches, and be 5'11". As a matter of fact, I realized quickly that I could live to be a hundred, but I would never be a "little old lady." No, I could do nothing to change my physical height. What some considered a liability, I accepted and began to consider an asset. When I found I could accept the things about myself I could not change, I was well on my way to laughing at myself and developing a sense of humor.

IDENTIFYING AND ACCEPTING YOUR UNIQUE CHARACTERISTICS

It is essential to have an accurate self-perception and to accurately perceive how other people view us. Some of our personal characteristics may be changeable, but we may not wish to do so. Whether these characteristics are changeable or not, it is important that we perceive ourselves as we really are and are able to laugh at our own idiosyncrasies and shortcomings.

All of us have some aspects of our features or personality that are unusual and may be funny if we look at them through humorous eyes. An honest self-evaluation has provided me with numerous opportunities to laugh at myself and have others laugh with me. For example . . .

- I am verrry su'thurn. One writer described my accent as being "as sweet as honeysuckle in spring" and said that I wrapped it around my audiences "like the scent of a magnolia tree in full bloom." (Sit down if you're getting queasy.)
- I weigh 160 pounds . . . on a good day.
- I'm not getting any younger. As I grow older, I'm just thankful wrinkles don't hurt.
- I am an atrocious housekeeper and cook. I do not clean house well, and I try to cook only one meal a year . . . Christmas dinner. After December 25th, I prefer to pack up the pots and pans with the decorations and put them away for another year.

These are just a few traits which are peculiar to me and which many people would view as liabilities. The magic comes in knowing ourselves, perceiving accurately how others see us, and accepting ourselves as we really are. The following anecdotes illustrate how accepting my unusual characteristics and viewing them with a humorous eye has helped me develop a sense of humor.

The Southern Advantage

Granted, I have a VERRY SU'THURN accent that seems to get more su'thurn as the years pass by, especially since I've found out . . . people will pay to hear su'thurn accents. And I would be less than honest if I did not admit that I have occasionally used this accent to my advantage.

Once I was scheduled to speak in Kingston, New York. I do not know what made me think I could drive out of Alamance County, North Carolina, to the Greensboro airport, fly to La Guardia, rent a car, drive myself out of New York City in rush hour traffic, get to Kingston, and reverse the process the next day.

I will not go into the details about the renting of the automobile. The person behind the counter did not speak southern. We were like little animals in a cage, looking at each other suspiciously. After repeated attempts to communicate, I said, "Just give me the little map. I'll pull over on the side of the road as I leave town, and find my own way out of New York City." Well, mark it down in your big book of important things to know. One does not pull over on the side of the road when leaving town, if the "town" is New York City.

A few minutes later, I found myself moving along in six lanes of traffic at 4:45 P.M. on my way out of The Big Apple. Suddenly, there were three bridges in front of me, and I had to make a choice. I could not even SEE the side of the road, and quickly realized I was not pulling over anywhere. A flash went through my body, and then I thought, "This might not be a bad time to use my southern accent."

I pulled into one of those toll booths that had a sign that meant, "If you do not have the EXACT CHANGE, come in here and talk to us." I rolled down my car window, looked up at the attendant and drawled in my very best southern, "Ay need sum helup."

He looked down at me as if to say, "We've got a live one right here."

"Is theus the rooad ta Kingstun, New Yoorrrk?" I drawled.

He answered in a very heavy New York accent, and his answer reminded me that it does not matter where people are from; basically, we can all be lumped into two categories: those who have a good sense of humor, and those who do not. He had a good one.

Leaning in toward me, he grinned and said, "Lady, not only IS 'dis da road to Kingston, but if you will wait a few minutes, I'll hold up da udda cars and give yous a HEAD START!"

With my head start I was able to make it out of the city and get to Kingston. That night after the speech, I thought about what this small-town person had done, and was right proud of myself. I was patting myself on the back a little too soon.

We can all look back at our lives and remember major accomplishments: graduations, the successful completion of an important project, or winning the championship game. When I approach the big lectern in the sky, and look back at the things of which I am very proud, this trip—especially the return—will certainly stand out.

As I drove back into the city the next day, I thought my life was going to end. I imagined the people back in Graham, North Carolina, saying, "That's what happens when you go to the biiiig city," but I was not so scared that I do not remember the experience. Certain things stand out: multiple lanes of traffic (even across a long bridge), everyone driving over the speed limit, lots of toll booths between Kingston and the airport (two at $1.25 each!), and coming out of toll booths like I was in the start of a race. My friend from the day before was nowhere to be seen.

Because I have been through this experience and have lived to tell about it, I believe it is my duty as a citizen to share some of what I learned in order that others, especially southerners from small towns, might benefit. I make the following suggestions:

1. Talk reeeeeeal sooooooutherrrrrn when you ask for directions at a toll booth. The operators immediately spot you as a potential hazard since you're not a native. Some will even slow down their talking and make sure you understand. They can do little about slowing down the traffic.

   Note: Pay NO ATTENTION to people who blow their horns at you while you are getting directions at a toll booth, or picking up the money you threw when you missed the man's hand. First come, first serve. Other people should learn to be more patient.

2. If you ask directions at a toll booth, do not just ask about a specific highway or turnoff. Ask WHICH LANE you should get in as soon as you come out of the starting blocks. GET IN THAT LANE and do not get out under ANY circumstances.

   Special note: Coming into La Guardia on the Grand Central Parkway from the north, get in the far right lane . . . not the most left.

   Additional note: Pay NO ATTENTION to people who blow their horns when you cross four lanes of traffic to move from the far most left lane to the far most right lane to make the La Guardia exit.

3. If you have to change lanes, DO NOT BOTHER to throw up your hand as a thank you when you move in front of someone. In most cases, they deserve no thanks. They did not let you in. You beat them to the spot, plain and simple, and a

hand thrown up is often interpreted as another type of gesture in New York City.

Note: Pay NO ATTENTION when people blow their horns as you throw up your hand at the car behind you. It is not your fault that they think you made an obscene gesture.

4. Back off from taxi drivers in ALL instances! It is their highway and they are very proud people. They will NOT back off in any situation, and are very likely to cut in front of you when there is no space, or follow so closely you believe they are trying to break into your trunk. Do not stop under any circumstances. Someone MAY break into your trunk.

Note: Shouting "Do you want me to tow you?" does no good when a taxi is right on the bumper of your car. Neither does blowing you horn nor throwing up your hand with appropriate emphasis . . . but it makes you feel like you belong.

Good Luck, y'all.

Weighing in at 160 Pounds

No step by step explanation of how I learned to accept my personal characteristics would be complete without a brief mention of my weight. I have tried to ignore it in the past, but it will not go away.

Fact: I weighed 160 pounds when I was thirteen, and I weigh 160 pounds now. This has been a struggle, and it is an accomplishment deserving recognition.

Second Fact: The 160 pounds is not necessarily located in the same places it was in when I was thirteen, or nineteen, or last year, for that matter. There has been a definite downward shift. (I always wanted dimples, but NOT on the sides of my legs.)

People know I weigh 160 pounds because . . . I tell them. I tell them because . . . they ask. For some reason, people want to know how much a 6′2″ woman weighs, so they ask. And then, they do not believe me.

A lady approached me after a speech and asked, "How MUCH did you say you weigh?"

"One hundred sixty pounds," I replied.

"Oh, you've got to be lying. You don't weigh any 160 pounds."

"If I were lying, I would not weigh 160 pounds," I assured her. "If I were lying, I would weigh more like . . . oh . . . how about 140 pounds?"

Long pause. "Well, you don't look like you weigh 160 pounds. Reeeeeally, you look like you weigh a hundred and forty, but then, you can carry it."

As Andy Griffith would say, "Now, don't that beat all? Don't that just beat all?" I can "carry it." I thought, "The next thing she will say is I'm big boned," but I smiled and said, "Let me know if you are aware of any way to ship it ahead. I have always figured, when I went, it went with me."

The Record Stands

Several years ago, I received a letter informing me a reporter would be calling for a brief interview for an article titled, "What Are They Doing Now?" It was a story about the last twenty-five Miss North Carolinas. I stopped and figured up the years. Yep, I was still included in the past twenty-five, but barely.

Several days later the call came. His questions were so routine that the thought crossed my mind that it would be nice not to be included in the past twenty-five and have to answer these questions again. "What was your first thought when you won the title of Miss North Carolina? Did you have a good time at the Miss America Pageant? What are some of your fondest memories about your year as Miss North Carolina?" I did not have the heart to tell him I barely remembered being Miss North Carolina.

Then he got to the nitty-gritty. "What I really want to know is what has happened to you over the years?"

"Ah, at last," I thought. "He wants to know what I have done SINCE I was in the Miss America Pageant. Hooray!" "Well . . . it was during my year as Miss North Carolina that I discovered I could make people laugh, which has evolved into a career as a professional speaker. I . . ."

"No," he interrupted. "I mean what has happened in regard to your body, your fitness, uh . . . your appearance. With the current craze in physical fitness, I plan to write this article from the slant of how former Miss North Carolinas have kept in shape."

I stopped walking around the kitchen with my long phone extension and sat down. This was serious.

He continued. "How would you say you look now compared to when you were Miss North Carolina?"

I was not about to let some young kid fresh out of journalism school get me down. "I look better," I answered quickly.

He laughed. "That's what everyone has said. Do you mind if I'm a little blunt?"

He had not been BLUNT up to that point?

"What do you weigh now, compared to what you weighed when you were Miss North Carolina?" he continued.

Now, I did not even know this fellow, and I figured he had a lot of nerve calling and asking questions about how much I weighed. His mother would gasp if she knew he was asking questions like that. I started to say that I had gained 350 pounds and worked at the state fair, and then I remembered that he was just a young reporter trying to do his job.

Suddenly it dawned on me. This young man really did not know anything about me. He did not know about my 6'2" height. He was just going down the list of Miss North Carolinas, probably wishing he had been assigned to cover the Duke-Carolina game.

"I tell you what," I said, grinning to myself. "I'll be honest. I weighed 160 pounds when I won the title of Miss North Carolina, and I weigh EXACTLY 160 pounds now."

There was a loooong silence. I thought he had gone away. Finally, he asked weakly, "Are you kidding?"

"No, son. I'm not."

After a few long, silent seconds, the astonished reporter cleared his throat and said, "Wellll, I guess that about answers all my questions."

Not Getting Any Younger

On another occasion I flew into Florida for a speech to a large corporation and was met at the airport by a junior executive from the company. He was a recent college graduate, about twenty-five years old, and was thrilled that he had been assigned this responsibility. All he had to do was meet the speaker and take her to the hotel to dine with the top executives and their spouses. He certainly wanted everything to come off without a hitch.

The drive to Boca Raton from the West Palm Beach airport takes about thirty minutes on a normal day. This day was not normal. When we got on the interstate, something was delaying traffic, and we came to a complete stop along with hundreds of other cars in all four lanes.

I could sense impatience creeping in on this fellow. He could see his job flashing before his eyes. Opening the door of the car, he stood on the floorboard leaning out to see as far ahead as possible. His body movements told me he was panicking. Pounding one's fist on the top of the car while shouting, "I can't believe this is happening," tends to be a giveaway.

Finally, he just could not stand it any longer. Pulling out of the line of traffic, he drove along the side of the highway . . . bumping on rocks, stirring up dust . . . and went right by all the other cars to the next exit ramp where we got off the interstate and detoured to the regular two-lane city streets. Of course, these streets had stoplights on every corner and were filled with local traffic, which only served to add to his frustration. He kept muttering, "I HATE to drive through these little sections because of the OLD people. They're all over the roads in Florida, peeking through their steering wheels, weaving from lane to lane." He was saying all these things while maneuvering our car in and out of traffic, scaring me to death, not to mention what he did to the "old people."

As we waited at one light, an elderly, white-haired gentleman fifty feet beyond our intersection began to slooowly drive his car onto the road, and bless his heart, he just could not seem to get the car out there. The light changed and my driver was going right toward him, saying "there's another one!" He sped up to the elderly man's car which was still creeping out, and then hit his brake. To my embarrassment, he sat on the horn while he said in disgust, "Would you look at that? Do you see what I mean?" He pounded his hand on the steering wheel. "They ought not to let anyone on the road who's over forty!" As soon as he said that, he remembered the age of the other person in the car, and in a quick instant, turned toward me and said, "Fifty-five!"

Notoriously Bad Housekeeper

We decided to surprise our son Beaver when he was eleven years old with a puppy for Christmas, and found just the one we wanted on December 18th. Because he was spending the week before Christmas with his grandparents, we kept the little dog at home until just before he returned on December 23rd. Our vet agreed to keep the pup until Christmas Eve night. We did not know the dog had deposited his calling card behind a chair in the den while he was with us.

The day before Christmas an old friend, Nancy Watson, dropped by, and I was showing her around our new home. Beaver had returned and tagged along. As we looked around the den, my friend caught sight of what had been left behind the chair. "I didn't know you had a dog," she commented. With my son standing nearby, I answered, "We don't." I was perplexed as to why she asked the question. She glanced behind the chair, shrugged her shoulders and said, "Oh."

It was not until a couple of days after Christmas when Nancy learned of our new puppy that she told me what she had seen. I could not believe it and asked, "What in the world did you think when I told you we did not have a dog?"

She replied, "I didn't think anything about it. The way you clean house, I figured the previous owner had left it there."

Redeye Gravy

My ability to cook is not much better than my ability to keep house. During one stage of my life, I certainly gave the kitchen its chance, but we just couldn't establish much of a rapport. One morning in particular stands out.

My husband loves country ham, grits, biscuits and that most southern of traditions—redeye gravy. I like them too, but prefer to order them at restaurants. Several days before a birthday of years past, I asked Jerry what he would like for a gift. It was the last time I gave the man a choice. He chose the items above, and placed special emphasis on the redeye gravy. He even added something like, "It can't be difficult to make, honey. A lot of people do it." "No problem," I assured him, and immediately telephoned my grandmother in Luverne, Alabama. Babies born in Luverne, Alabama, are given the recipe for redeye gravy when they leave the hospital.

Although I was hesitant, my grandmother assured me it was quite easy and gave me the following directions: "Fry the ham in a frying pan until brown, take the ham out and pour the grease in a little bowl, leaving the browned drippings in the pan. Add a tablespoon or two of coffee to the drippings in the frying pan, heat and pour into the grease, making the red eye in the redeye gravy."

Well, it certainly sounded simple to me. Unfortunately, however, if you read back over her directions, you'll notice she did not say anything about first cooking the coffee.

I cooked the ham and set it to the side. Measured out two heaping tablespoons of coffee grinds and dumped them in the drippings in the frying pan. A few minutes later I spooned the concoction out of the frying pan, put it into the grease, and proceeded to put the "gravy" all over the top of the biscuits. I was so proud when I put it in front of Jerry and said, "Happy Birthday."

Looking back on it, I'll say one thing for him. He tried. He really tried to eat those biscuits that were covered in a very unusual, gritty redeye gravy. And of course, I watched with pride and soon asked, "Well, what do you think?"

"It's different," he said, chewing very slowly.

"Different? What do you mean?"

"I'm not sure," he mumbled, and slowly worked his tongue around in his mouth. "But it's the first time I have ever had redeye gravy stuck in between my teeth."

SHARING YOUR BLOOPERS, BLUNDERS, AND PUT-DOWNS

We are often afraid to laugh at our mistakes, errors, or blunders: the things we do which we believe make us look irresponsible or foolish. Those around us realize this inability to laugh at our mistakes as quickly as they realize the foible.

By sharing stories about our biggest errors or blunders, we begin to break down the barriers thrown up by refusing to laugh at ourselves. Consider the words of Gascoigne, "An error gracefully acknowledged is a victory won. To make mistakes is human; to stumble is commonplace; to be able to laugh at yourself is maturity." Thomas Fuller observed, "He is not laughed at, that laughs at himself first."

I have always found a few opening words help me ease into sharing my mistakes with friends in a humorous way. Questions or phrases such as "You won't believe what I have done!" or "If they don't come and take me away this time, they're missing their best chance," permit me to ease into telling my error. Telling the error is a step toward laughing at myself.

During my nine years of teaching and coaching, I found it a relief to share with fellow educators some of the ridiculous things I did. In most instances I learned others had done the same things, and we laughed together. More importantly, I was continuing to learn to laugh at myself by sharing stories about my blunders.

I now do that same thing with my fellow professional speakers. Most of the time I travel by myself. When I make a blunder, and there are plenty of them, it tends to settle in my throat in a little knot that seems to grow. When I bump into another speaker and share the mistake, or talk to my family about what happened, the supposed knot disappears.

Being able to share experiences when we have been put down by others is particularly important. Although this is not easy, it is one of the most important aspects of a good sense of humor. There also may be occasions when we receive recognition or special attention which tend to give us an exaggerated feeling of self-importance and we deserve to be put down. On these occasions, in particular, we need to be able to share put-downs we receive from others. Sharing these occasions may be the ultimate in having a good sense of humor.

Here are some examples from my travels and experiences where bloopers, blunders, and put-downs have been the basis for stories that brought laughter to others. More importantly, by sharing these with others, I have further developed the magic of laughing at myself.

Etiquette Faux Pas

The week after I won the title of Miss North Carolina, two women began to work with me to get me ready to go to the Miss America Pageant . . . to lose. They said that they had never worked with as much raw material. At first, we worked on walking and talking and similar things that they believed needed significant improvement, but after watching me at a reception, they quickly turned their attention toward the rules of etiquette.

The lesson in etiquette occurred the first time I was introduced to the thick, red plastic around cheese. Unfortunately, I did not realize it was plastic. I cut off a wedge of cheese and put it in my mouth, plastic cover and all, and started trying to eat it. The plastic stuck to my top teeth and embedded in my bottom teeth, holding my mouth almost shut tight. I stood there, trying to chew and make idle chitchat from behind my locked jaws. I was thinking, "This is TOUGH CHEESE." Others must have been thinking, "This woman is a nut!"

After the reception the powers that be decided to go over a few areas other than walking and talking. This bothered my mother because she thought she had done a fairly good job teaching me about such things, but when she heard about the plastic cheese, she sighed and told the ladies, "Do what you can." In a matter of weeks, I learned more etiquette than I ever cared to know, but I quickly found out that I did not learn everything.

It is not that growing up in Graham, North Carolina, I had never HEARD of a finger bowl. I had heard of a finger bowl. It is just that we do not use them EVERYDAY in Graham. To be truthful, at that point in my life my eyes had never seen a finger bowl. I guess if I had ever thought about it, I would have thought a finger bowl would be about the size of something to put your fingers in. I would have never dreamed it is a bowl about four inches across, and that it is filled with water so people can wash their fingers after eating at very formal meals. I certainly would not have thought about it having a lemon in it to assist in cutting the grease off one's hands.

Several months after all the etiquette lessons began, I was the guest of honor at a formal banquet at a very exclusive country club in Greensboro, North Carolina. As the honored guest, I sat at the center of the head table with people to my right and left. As soon as I saw the situation, my head started working like a computer. Etiquette. Etiquette. I had been taught that as the person at the center of the head table, everyone would wait until I began to eat before they started.

I tried out what I had learned during the first courses. Each time a course was brought in, I smiled at the people on my right, and I smiled at the people on my left, and when everyone was served, I started . . . and they followed suit. Everything clicked along smoothly through about five courses, and by then, my Graham, North Carolina, stomach told me it was time for dessert.

At that point, the waitress brought in a bowl about four inches wide, and put it right down in front of me. I want to get one thing straight. I AM NOT A FOOL. It LOOKED like water to me, but it had that LEMON floating around down in there. I thought to myself that this must be some new type of lemon dessert.

I smiiiled while they served the people on my right, and I smiiiled while they served the people on my left, and I picked up my spoon . . . and dove right in.

. . . Three people at the head table picked up their spoons and dove right in, too.

Since that unforgettable occasion, my career as a professional speaker has afforded me the opportunity to attend literally thousands of banquets. In all my years of travel, I have never seen another finger bowl. I do not know whether this one place in Greensboro is the only place still using them, or . . . the word spread that "she does not know what one is."

Realistic Value

The meeting was at the convention center in Winston-Salem, so I drove over from Burlington. Upon arrival, I went into the ladies room to freshen up before going down to the banquet. I was at a mirror around the corner from the main door when two women attending the convention came in and started talking about the evening's activities. After a few minutes, they got around to the program.

"Who's gonna speak tonight?"

"I dunno. I'd leave after the meal, but I want a chance at winning that TV they're giving away."

"Well, me too. I'll sit through ANYBODY for a chance at a television."

I just couldn't resist the opportunity. From around the corner I said, "I've heard the speaker. She's very good."

Silence.

I continued. "She's a former Miss North Carolina from Graham . . . she's funny."

One of them said, "What's wrong with her?"

"Not that kind of funny. She tells stories and plays the ukulele."

More silence, until one of them finally asked the other, "Is it a COLOR TV?"

Hams to Go

I like the folks "down east" in North Carolina. Basically, they are a bunch of good ol' boys and girls of all ages—loose, down-home folks. I would probably fit in well if I ever lived there. They do anything for their friends . . . and do not mind asking a friend to do something for them.

The request I received from one meeting planner in eastern North Carolina might have taken aback some of my speaker friends in California, or Boston, or any of the other big-city-type places in which most of them live; especially, if they had begun thinking that being paid high fees to speak made them more important.

I was booked to speak at a farm-type banquet. Air travel was out of the question, and my plans called for leaving home around lunch for the 3-to-4 hour drive.

The phone rang mid-morning. It was the fella in charge of

the whole shindig. "Jeanne, you drivin' down this afternoon, aren't you?"

We had sent our usual speaker's check list with travel plans. He knew I was driving down. I recognized opening chitchat, and wondered why he called.

"Sure am. I'll probably get there around five o'clock and go straight to the community college. Starts at six, doesn't it?"

"Yep. Six." There was a pause. "You coming through Raleigh?"

More chitchat. Through Raleigh was the only way to get there. He was leading up to something.

"Look," he continued. "We're giving away twenty country hams tonight, and the outfit that's donating 'em is in Raleigh. How 'bout stopping over and picking 'em up. It'd save somebody down here a trip."

"Do you want me to come early and set the tables?" I joked.

He laughed. "Naw, but we shore would 'preciate it if you could pick up them hams. Our people really look forward to getting those hams every year."

He would do the same for me or anybody else. That is just the way we do things here in North Carolina. "No problem," I told him, and got the directions.

It turned out that "pickin' up them hams" meant adding about an hour and a half to my trip, which meant I had to scurry around and leave right away. The ham place turned out to be off the beaten path. I hit downtown traffic in Raleigh and took a few wrong turns, but finally found the building.

There was one high school boy on the premises there to load the hams. When I looked at my watch and calculated how long it would take me . . . I started assisting with the loading process. The hams were like big, heavy babies and the process was slow—one at time . . . from the building out to the car. After six hams, the phone rang and the teenager left to answer it. He was gone a loooong time, and I had the hams about loaded when he returned—very clever boy.

Outside Raleigh it started raining, and I do mean RAINING. A few miles further, I had to pull off the road. Timewise, I knew I would be cutting it close, and I was getting nervous. A speaker takes a lot of pride in getting to bookings on time. I called and left word I was on the way and forged ahead.

I pulled into town at six o'clock on the nose. I knew the chairman would be in a state of panic. Where was his speaker? What would he do to entertain 300 farmers if she did not get there? Could she have been in an accident?

It was still raining when I pulled on the community college campus. Knowing how relieved he would be to see me . . . I did not even look for a parking place, but instead, pulled right up to the front door. The rain stopped beating on the car as I pulled under the breezeway. I could see all the people inside at the customary long tables covered with white butcher's paper. They were already digging into the North Carolina barbecue.

As I gathered my purse and ukulele, someone tapped on the car window. I rolled it down to see a man, brow wrinkled with concern, staring me right in the face. "Are you Jeanne?" he asked.

"Yes."

He turned toward the building and shouted, "It's her!"

From off in the distance I could hear sprinkled applause and I knew that they were relieved that I had arrived. As a matter of fact, people seemed excited to see me. The speaker was on the premises. Everyone could relax. No one would have to step in with an extemporaneous program.

I must admit it felt good for my arrival to generate such excitement . . . until . . . I stepped out of the car and several voices in the distance shouted, "HAS SHE GOT THEM HAMS?"

It's Your Turn to Work Magic

Take a good look at yourself and identify characteristics that may be considered by others as unusual, different, or even liabilities. These may be physical characteristics that are unchangeable or other traits that you may not wish to change. Look at each of these characteristics with humorous eyes and discover that the ability to laugh at yourself is the most important ingredient in the recipe for developing a sense of humor.

Now turn to your own personal experiences. There are bound to be some bloopers or blunders or times that you were put down that stand out in your home, social, or business activities. Make some notes about your favorite ones . . . especially those that you believe would be worthy to tell, and equally important, that you would feel comfortable telling. Plan to have fun. Be assured there will always be occasions in family, social, or business gatherings when one of your experiences will fit . . . and you can be the center of wit and wisdom. It's one potion for applying "The Magic of Genie" as you develop your sense of humor.

Potion 2
Look for the Humor
in Everyday Situations

One of the biggest differences between those who possess a keen sense of humor and those who do not is that humor-oriented people observe the humorous happenings that occur around them while others seem oblivious to the funny side of life. Therefore, it is essential that people intent on enhancing their sense of humor develop the ability to look for humor in everyday situations.

Humor is certainly abundant in our everyday experiences. It is found in all aspects of our lives: from home life, especially the uninhibited thoughts and actions of children; the classroom, with the maturing process and its problems; the work place, particularly the miscues and plain ridiculous things that are said or done; in sports, among the losers and the winners; in traveling, among the people struggling against the waves of others travelers trying to cope with schedules, delays, reservations, lost baggage, and a myriad of other related issues. Humor also abounds in politics and government . . . as Will Rogers said about his greatest source of humor: "I guess it wouldn't be very humorous if it wasn't for government. I don't make jokes, I just watch the government and report the facts."

Since our daily events are rich with humor, it is not necessary to search for jokes or humorous material to bring smiles to our faces as we strive to enhance our humor; it is all around us. The magic trick is to recognize witty or funny experiences when we see or hear them.

Let me share some of the everyday situations I have experienced over the years, situations I deem to be amusing, and in some cases, downright funny. But I hasten to point out that I noticed them because I was looking for them. Anyone can look for humor in everyday situations and find it.

In order for me to share anecdotal examples from my everyday situations, you must know a little more about the crazy world of professional speaking. According to the American Society of Association Executives, there are over a million paid speeches given in the United States every year. These presentations are made at a variety of events from national conventions and corporate meetings to local chamber of commerce banquets. In many cases, the speaker is an in-house person or a politician; in other instances, the speaker is a celebrity. But a very large number of those speaking slots are filled by professional speakers. In most cases, we are not celebrities, although generally well-known by meeting planners and our children's friends. We fall into certain categories: trainers, keynoters, workshop leaders, and consultants, to name a few. Most speakers specialize in specific areas: i.e., real estate, finance, motivation, stress management, time management, etc., and (sound the trumpet!) . . . there are the humorists! I "are" one of those.

Humorists should not be confused with comedians or come-diennes, whose only objective is to make the audience laugh and often use off-color material and four-letter words to achieve that objective. While humorists may be just as funny, they generally use clean humor to illustrate certain points.

This sums up what I do for a living. It also explains why my everyday situations—where I look for humor—may differ from those of many individuals. The main portion of my workday is spent traveling from one speech to another. Much of my time is spent on airplanes and in airports. After I arrive in a city, I switch to other charming modes of transportation such as cabs, vans, limos, buses, trains, and rental cars for the final miles to my lodging. With that travel behind me, I begin to work with the happy personnel at hotels, motels, resorts, and convention centers. Finally, usually after hours of travel, I find myself in speaking situations ranging from the magnificent ballrooms in state of the art convention facilities to pig pickin's held out-doors in the pouring rain.

When I first began to make a conscious practice of looking for humor, it certainly was not for the purpose of working on my sense of humor. I was searching for humorous material to use in my speeches. As a humorist, I learned a long time ago there is no need for me to spend time making up funny stories when I have the whole world to write them for me. Airline and hotel person-nel, cab drivers, other travelers, speaking situations, neighbors, and indeed my own family, do and say much funnier things than I could ever create. All I had to do was develop my humor awareness. When I did, I found I had an abundance of material for my speeches—material that came from life's experiences, not joke books. And as I gathered humorous speech material, I realized I was enjoying my day-to-day work more. In short, I was enhancing my own sense of humor. Here are some examples of humor I found when I made it a priority to open my eyes and ears and look for it.

Confusion Delusion

I had already taken my seat on a flight out of Washington when a gentleman boarded the plane and sat down next to me. We exchanged a few cordial remarks, and before long he asked the usual, "What do you do for a living?"

"I'm a professional speaker."

His eyes widened and he turned halfway around in his seat in order to see me better. He thought I said "professional STREAKER." "No kidding?" he managed to get out, in disbelief.

I nodded.

"Where do you do this?"

"Oh, all over the country," I replied. "At sales meetings, conventions, or banquets. Anywhere a group of people get together."

He grew silent and straightened himself in his seat. His mind was racing.

Mine was, too. I wondered what was wrong with the fellow. Being a professional speaker is not THAT unusual.

A few minutes went by, but he just could not remain silent. Turning back toward me, he took up the conversation as though we had never stopped talking. "And people PAY you to do this?"

What IS his problem? I thought. "I'm paid a fee plus expenses," I answered.

He looked at the rings on my left hand. "I notice you're married."

"Yes," I said matter-of-factly.

"May I ask what your husband thinks about you doing this?"

"Oh," I smiled. "He's proud of me. He enjoys seeing me in front of people."

This conversation took place at the beginning of a cross-country flight. Therefore, after a couple of hours of perplexed looks, the passenger and I did straighten it out that I am a professional speaker, not streaker. He was greatly relieved. As a matter of fact, he said that at one point when I had gone to the back of the plane, he was scared to death I was going to come "flashing" up the aisle . . . and everyone would think I was with him.

But while he had been shocked by what he at first thought was my occupation, he was equally as fascinated by what I really do for a living. He asked all the standard questions about speaking—how professional speakers obtain bookings, organize speeches, gather material, and select topics—but he was most intrigued by the amount of travel associated with my work. To quote him, "I do not see how you can STAND all that traveling, checking in and out of hotels, and that banquet food! How do you put up with all the hassles?"

Not only do I put up with all the hassles associated with my career, I enjoy them because I make a concentrated effort to look for the humor in everyday situations. Being aware of the humor in everyday situations has been invaluable in enhancing my sense of humor.

The Spokin' Words

Traveling to one speaking engagement, I got on an airplane—at 6'2", that is not my easiest thing to do—and was standing on the jetway behind the other passengers. I could hear the flight attendant at the plane door telling everybody, "Watch your st'ep." She was from the South. Two syllables. "St'ep." When I got up there, she changed it. "Watch your he'ad."

Well, I did watch my "he'ad." I got on the plane, and was sitting there minding my own business when a man came on the plane in a three-piece, dress-for-success suit. He was carrying a matching briefcase that made it a four-piece suit. I glanced down, and for the life of me, I could not tell where the legs of the pants ended and the briefcase started. Of course, he sat down next to me, and after a while he asked what people always ask on airplanes, "What do you do for a living?"

With the professional streaker episode fresh in my my mind, I was careful to enunciate. "I am a professional SPEAKER."

He was busy putting his look alike brief case under the seat in front of him, but he stopped, looked me straight in the eyes, and said, "Well, you don't look like a professional speaker."

I smiled. "I've been sick."

My seat companion broke out laughing, and I settled back to await the flight attendant and pilot announcements. If you are looking for humor, these are always good places to find it.

At the beginning of one trip, the flight attendant was in the middle of routine announcements when she mistakenly said, "Only lightweight passengers are permitted in the overhead compartments." I looked around to see if anyone else caught it, but most people were engrossed in their newspapers or were asleep. As in most instances, unfortunately, some of the best humor goes over people's heads because they are not looking for it in travel situations—like the time the flight attendant announced, "Ladies and gentlemen, please leave your seat belts fastened until you've walked into the gate area," or " . . . and ladies and gentlemen, I would like to remind you that your bottom is removable, and may be used as a floatation device." Could she have meant your seat cushion?

Folks need a long vacation when they do not see something a little humorous about an elegantly dressed gentleman, carrying an expensive leather brief case, boarding a plane with a Snoopy bag slung over his shoulder; or grown men and women, armed with brief cases and portable computers, in the Delta Crown Room in Atlanta on a Saturday morning trying to decide whether to watch Elmer Fudd or the Roadrunner. How about the passenger wearing earphones who does not realize he is joining in—out loud and at the top of his lungs—on every chorus of "You Picked A Fine Time To Leave Me, Lucille"? You cannot make up things like this, or the other travel experiences that follow . . . .

Deceiving Appearance

During one trip, I was seated in an aisle seat on a crowded plane waiting for a flight to depart to Dearborn, Michigan. A woman boarded with a two-year-old child and sat in the center seat beside me. She put the child in her lap, and the little girl began to twist and turn. I commented to the mother, "When they shut the door, if there is an empty seat ANYWHERE, I'll move and you can put your little girl in this seat." The lady thought I was especially nice, but in truth, I DON'T LIKE TO SIT NEXT TO SQUIRMING CHILDREN. They crawl all over you.

As soon as the door was shut, I practically leaped to the one remaining seat several rows behind me. An elderly gentleman, whom I later found out to be eighty-five years old, was sitting beside the empty seat and had placed his hat in it. "I'm sorry," I commented, "but if I move here, a young mother will not have to hold her daughter the entire trip." He smiled, nodded his head, and picked up his hat.

As I sank into the seat, I added under my breath, "Not only that, but I don't like someone crawling all over me during the trip."

The eighty-five year old gentleman looked up and with a glint in his eye said, "Weelllll . . . I make no promises."

Sick Bag

As soon as an elderly lady sat in the window seat next to me on one flight, she immediately pulled out an airsick bag from the seat compartment in front of her. We were still on the ground, but she quickly flipped the bag open, held it in both hands, and started peering inside as though she was going to be sick any moment.

I moved slightly in the other direction. "Are you all right?"

"I don't feel well," she said weakly, still peering into the bag.

"Would you like for me to get the flight attendant?"

"Yes, darling, I think you'd better." Poor thing.

I pushed the call button, and the flight attendant was by our seats in a matter of seconds. She saw the situation immediately. How could she help but . . . here was this sweet-looking, little elderly lady clutching an airsick bag.

"Ma'am, can I help you?"

The lady never looked up from the bag. "I feel a little weak."

The attendant asked, "Would you like something to drink?"

With that question, the lady turned her face toward us and in a pitiful little voice said, "I believe a scotch and water on the rocks will help."

We were in the coach section, and the plane was still on the ground. Drinks were not to be served in that situation, but I watched in amazement as the attendant went up the aisle and brought back the drink. No charge.

"I believe I'll be all right now," the little hustler said as she took the drink. When the flight attendant left, poor granny turned to me and said, "It works EVERY time."

I wonder how old one has to be . . . .

A Traveling Dog

I was already seated on an aircraft when a passenger boarded with a Seeing Eye dog. All of the flight attendants were hustling around, but one quickly helped him to his seat.

In a few minutes, a stomach-laden, good ol' boy dressed in boots and jeans, walked to the front of the plane and drawled to a second attendant who evidently had not seen the animal board the plane, "Ma'am, I'm sittin' next to a dawg back there. Be all right if I change seats?"

The young woman snapped, "You're no prize yourself, buddy, but if you don't want to sit next to her, move."

Executive Dilemma

I had already boarded a flight out of Ft. Lauderdale when the gate agent came on board to talk to the man seated across the aisle from me. The agent told the passenger that upon checking his ticket they discovered his reservation was for the 25th, the next day. The man slammed down the newspaper he was reading. "That secretary! Another mistake! She cannot do ANYTHING right!" His voice carried halfway through the plane. "This is the last straw!"

The gate agent assured him there was no problem. Seats were available on this and his connecting flight, but not the seats that he thought he had been assigned. The agent gave him his new seat assignments and left.

Out of the corner of my eye, I could see this fellow just sitting there . . . thinking. In a few minutes, he quietly gathered his things and headed for the front of the plane. As he passed the door, a flight attendant said, "Everything's been worked out, sir. The gate agent switched your ticket to today."

Very subdued, the man mumbled, "Actually, I'm supposed to be going tomorrow."

Solo Charter

I arrived at the airport in Huntsville, Alabama, around 7:45 A.M. for a nine o'clock flight. Passing the United Airlines counter, I noticed their 6:30 A.M. flight had "delayed" written next to it. Jokingly I said to the counter agent, "Your flight to Atlanta is not delayed an hour and a half is it, say until now?" He grinned, "It sure is. Take off. Gate 5."

I hurriedly called my client, who was meeting me at the airport in Atlanta, and told him I was changing airlines and would be arriving early. I offered to take a cab, but the gentleman insisted, "I'll be there to meet you."

When I arrived at the gate, the agent was laughing. "So you're the lady who's chartered this flight? We've been waiting for you." It turned out that all of the other scheduled passengers had switched off the delayed flight to another carrier, and I was it. As a matter of fact, the crew was getting ready to fly the plane back to Atlanta when I approached the ticket counter.

"Where would you like to sit?" the gate agent asked.

"It sounds as though I have my choice."

"Not really, we need you in the back for weight." (Funny man.)

As I walked toward the plane, the pilots waved and all three attendants greeted me at the door and rolled out the carpet. I took my seat—in the back to balance the pilots and attendants in the front, of course—and surveyed all the empty seats in front of me. It was a weird feeling. Three pilots, three flight attendants, and me, on a jet airplane that seated something like ninety-six. I was sitting waaaaay in the back all by myself, surveying rows and rows of empty seats and thinking, "Boy, if the people in Graham, North Carolina, could see this . . . they would fall over laughing." In just a few minutes, the pilot came over the P.A. system and boomed, "Welcome aboard, Mrs. Robertson. If you're ready to go, we'll leave in just a few minutes." I waved back, and with all the southern grace and charm instilled by my genteel mother, shouted, "Let her rip!"

It was a great trip. I have been on many chartered flights, even several chartered corporate jets, but a chartered commercial flight? No, this was a first. I felt like I should be from Texas.

It has often been said that you can take the girl out of the country, but you can't take the country out of the girl. Halfway through the flight, when all the attendants were up front talking, I could not resist reaching up and pulling the flight attendant call button . . . just to make sure they did not forget me.

We arrived in Atlanta, and I stood at the gate telling my new friends good-bye and that I certainly enjoyed my chartered flight. One of the pilots even said, "The next time you want to charter a commercial jet, think of United."

Unbeknownst to me, my client, who had booked me on a fee plus expenses basis, was standing nearby listening to our parting comments. When I turned to walk toward him, he blurted out, "WHAT IN THE WORLD WILL THIS COST US?"

Perky and Particular

During one flight I found myself seated next to a very dressed-up young lady about six years old. I could tell much time and thought had gone into coordinating her traveling outfit. She was very feminine—we would have said "prissy" a few years ago—and sat quietly holding her little purse while her feet dangled.

Mid-way through the flight, the attendant came by and offered her a pair of wings, a comic book, and a deck of playing cards that was wrapped in cellophane with the usual red pull tab.

The little girl looked at the gifts a few seconds and smoothed out the skirt of her dress before answering in a prim and proper manner, "I'd like the wings and the book, but I DO NOT SMOKE!"

Child Wisdom

I travel through the Atlanta airport almost every other day, and I am accustomed to the "people mover" system there. When the passengers board the train system, if the door is held up from closing, a recording quickly cuts on that says in a Darth Vader-type voice, "YOUR DEPARTURE IS BEING DELAYED BECAUSE SOMEONE IS STANDING IN THE DOORWAY." The voice is accompanied by a sound similar to a laser gun shooting through the air, and it does several things: (1) clears the doorway, (2) creates a few chuckles, or (3) scares people to death.

The Houston Intercontinental airport has something similar to prevent travelers from taking airport-owned luggage carts out of specified areas. During one trip I was transferring from one terminal to another on the moving train system. At the first stop, I watched a family push one of the grocery-like carts piled high with their luggage onto the train. The parents had their hands full with a young boy and a baby, and the bags and sacks that naturally accompany such an entourage during a family vacation. The doors shut and then quickly opened while a recorded message barked, "THE ELECTRONIC SECURITY DEVICE HAS DETECTED A ROLLING CART ON BOARD. PLEASE PUT IT OFF!"

The father and the little boy started slinging bags off the cart while the mother wrestled with diaper bags and a squirming baby. The rest of us tried to help by pushing bags to the side when they hit the floor. It was as though we were racing against flood waters. After a minute or so of frantic effort, the father pushed the empty cart off the train, and everybody sank into seats. The doors shut and we were on our way.

The first stop was a parking area. The doors opened, and stayed open, and staaaayed open. We sat . . . and sat. After a few minutes the little boy said, "Daddy, if the man could see we had the cart on the train, why can't he see that nobody wants to get off here?"

First Class Travel

At the beginning of one trip, I noticed one of the flight attendants had a big, new teddy bear on board and had strapped it in one of the front seats. When a passenger needed that space, she quietly unlocked the bear and put it in the overhead baggage storage area. No one commented about it.

During the flight a lady requested some information about the frequent flyer program. The flight attendant started answering her questions, stopped and said, "Wait, I'm confused."

A man seated nearby said, "If you think YOU are confused, think how the bear feels in the dark."

Crystal-Gazer

Anyone who has traveled lately realizes that in most cases a limousine is actually a van. I was one of two passengers in the limo from the Savannah, Georgia airport to Hilton Head Island where I was scheduled to speak at a convention. The driver was a personable fellow and obviously a frustrated tour guide. His running commentary started as we pulled away from the airport curb. He said that he could tell by the way people acted in the limo what type of group they were with and why they were going to Hilton Head. "If they stop at the convenience store for setups," he said, "I know they're here to party. If they have golf clubs, I know they're here to play golf. If they have brief cases and pull out papers, I know they're here to work." "Of course," he added with a laugh, "if they sit in the back of the limo and count their money, I know they are doctors."

He looked at me in the rear view mirror and asked, "What do you do for a living?" I told him I was a professional speaker. His face clouded over. He didn't know anything about professional speaking, so he shifted his eyes in the mirror and repeated the question to the man seated behind me.

This fellow had been sitting there quietly during the entire ride. He looked back at the driver in the mirror and said pleasantly, "I'm a doctor . . . hundred thousand one, hundred thousand two."

Twas Hawg-Wild

For years, when I have been in taxis, I have asked the driver several what I call "humor searching questions." I generally start the conversation by just nonchalantly asking, "How long have you been driving a cab?" The drivers say something like, "Oh, twenty-five years. Yep, been driving twenty-five years." (Cab drivers repeat themselves a lot.)

We ride along a few seconds, and then I say, "Boy, I bet you've seen some funny things happen in your cab during all those years."

"Oh yea. I could write a book. COULD WRITE A BOOK."

At that point I let them think for a few seconds before zeroing in. "What's the funniest thing that's ever happened in your cab?"

I do not always get hilariously funny things when I go through this procedure. Once a driver even snapped back, "Don't want nothing FUNNY happening in this cab. That's why I don't drive at night!" Of course, I get a lot of stories that are not funny at all. But once in a while . . . I'll get a winner.

I was taking a cab from the hotel to the airport in Spartanburg, South Carolina. It was early in the morning, but I decided to get things rolling and ask my questions.

"How long you been driving a cab?"

"Seventeen years. Seven . . . teen years."

I waited.

"Boy, I bet you've had some funny things happen in a cab in seventeen years?"

"Oh yea. You wouldn't believe it, lady. You just wouldn't believe it."

I waited a little longer.

"What's the funniest thing you've ever had happen in your cab?"

The driver thought a few seconds and drawled, "Weeeelllll. It coulda been that time I had that hawg as a fare?"

I knew I had a winner, and being from the South, I knew a "hawg" was a BIG PIG. "A hog?"

"Yep. I got a call from a fella down here out from town and when I got down there . . . it turned out he wanted me to take his big ol' hawg down to his brother's at the other end of the

county. I didn't much want to do it, but I got to thinking and I figured
. . . a fare's a fare."

I nodded.

"It took the two of us to get the thing into the back seat. It was huge . . . BIG snout . . . BIG pointed, floppy ears. And it didn't want to go for a ride in a cab. It spread its feet up against the outside of the doors and all, but we finally got it in the back seat, and the fella paid me the fare . . . and me and hawg was off. I reckon if I had to say so, that would be the funniest thing that has ever happened in this cab. That hawg sat right up in the back seat like it had good sense, looking out the windows. People riding by us ran off the road. People coming toward us hit their brakes. Yep," he chuckled. "That was funny all right."

"Well, tell me something else. Would you do it again?"

"Nope. Nope, I wouldn't do it again," he said, shaking his head. "Not again."

I leaned forward. "It messed up your cab, didn't it?"

"Naw, that wasn't it atall. You see, the thing is . . . hawgs don't tip."

Then he caught my eye in the rear view mirror and grinned. "But ladies do . . . ."

The Lodging Challenge

We have always found it easier for my clients to make the room reservation for me, usually at the place where the meeting will be held. But I am a humorous speaker and my audiences are not limited to one type of event. One day I may speak at a national convention held in the finest resort hotel in the country and stay right there; while the next day I may be booked to speak at a chamber of commerce banquet in the smallest of towns and stay with a family in the area. I just never know, and to be honest, I thrive on the variety.

One trip I may be in the $2500-a-night presidential suite at the Sheraton in Scottsdale, Arizona, and the very next night be in a motel room where the bed and air conditioner are supported by concrete blocks. On occasion I may be in a hotel where the amenities include shampoo, conditioner, hair spray, lotion, shoe buffers, and a variety of other toiletries; as well as candy and liqueurs left on the bedside table by the person who hides in the hall and sneaks into your room to turn down your bed as soon as you leave. The next night I may just as well be in a hotel where the only amenity . . . is hot water.

Many times I have arrived at my lodging very late at night, tired and hungry, to discover room service is not available because there is no restaurant connected to the hotel; or that the restaurant closed five minutes before I arrived and the nearest food is a couple of blocks away. In this situation I have had a desk clerk say, "I wouldn't walk it this time of night, but you can give it a try." Of course, in a similar situation the next night, it is very likely a basket of fruit will be waiting for me in my room, compliments of the hotel staff.

I have dealt with bell captains who wrestled me to the sidewalk to take one little bag out of my hand, and assured me it would be in the room when I got there. This usually means that they know something I am about to find out; I will not be able to get into my room for several hours. I have left wake up calls with many mysterious people who just happened to walk through the hotel office and talk to me . . . never to be seen or heard from again, and of course, never to write down my wake up time.

I stayed in a hotel in Oklahoma that was in the process of being remodeled and had no mirrors. No mirrors! Think about getting ready in the morning without any mirrors. The desk clerk said, "You're lucky. The commodes just came in last week." I have been in a rush in the wee dark hours of the morning, packing my bag to get to a flight out of Chicago, when all the lights in the hotel went off. Try feeling your way down nine fights of steps in total darkness, all the time wondering what you left in the room because you could not see to pack. I have slept in a double bed with the president of a state woman's club whom I had never met before that night. (She had forgotten to get the speaker a room.) I have been next door to more hospitality suites than I can count, and when you are trying to sleep at 2:00 A.M., these suites are not so hospitable.

BELIEVE ME, when you travel much of the time, what it boils down to is service. It did not take me long to figure out that sometime the service is better in a ten-room motel than in a high-rise hotel. Room service that will be delivered in twenty minutes, beats placing a breakfast order at 7:00 A.M. and being asked, "Ya want it 'dis morning?" When a traveler is tired, a person with a smile behind the check-in desk is more important than a row of uninterested clerks in stiff uniforms. Regardless of the surroundings, "Your room is ready, Mrs. Robertson," is always better than, "I'm sorry, Mrs. Robertson, but at this time, we are underdeparted." Underdeparted? Give me a break.

The more I travel, the more familiar I become with various places to stay across the United States and Canada. I know when I check into the Hershey Convention Center in Hershey, Pennsylvania, the desk clerk is going to give me a big chocolate bar; when I check into a certain motel in one small southern town, the desk clerk is going to give me a fly swatter; and when I stay in a certain hotel during the winter season, it will be so cold that I must sleep with the chair cushions on top of me. Through it all, I have learned that if I do not look for the humor in these situations, I am very likely to jump out the window of one of those high rises one night . . . and take their seat cushions with me.

Information Please

On a trip into Tulsa, two of the flight attendants were discussing where they wanted to eat dinner that night. They had heard of a restaurant called the Cajun Wharf, but did not know where it was located. Another passenger told them he had heard it was great, but he could not help them with directions. They asked several other people for the information, but to no avail.

Finally, one of the attendants clicked on the P.A. system and said, "Attention, ladies and gentlemen. If anyone on board knows the location of the restaurant in Tulsa named the Cajun Wharf, please raise your hand." Several hands shot up. "Thank you," she said, and proceeded up the aisle to get the information.

A very excited woman several rows in front of me touched her on the arm and said, "Excuse me, Miss, but would you mind asking if anybody knows the name of a good, cheap motel?"

Bewitched

With a great deal of apprehension, I approached the desk at a very grand hotel in Victoria, British Columbia, late at night. I had a guaranteed reservation, but my flight had run late and I was fearful my room would be gone. It was around 1:00 A.M.

After I gave my name, the desk clerks huddled together and kept glancing my way. I was prepared for them to tell me the worst, but no, after a few minutes they told me there was a parlor room available with a sofa that made into a bed. That was fine with me.

I had been in the room just a few minutes when I noticed a cigar burning in the ashtray on an end table. While I was looking at it, I heard someone moving around behind a door off the parlor. I froze, and after a few frightful seconds, managed to call out, "Who's there?" The movement stopped. No one answered. I was scared and don't know what made me pull a bluff. "Identify yourself, or I'll call the police!" I shouted, trying to sound courageous.

Silence.

So much for courageous. Panicking, I called the front desk and told them what had happened. After a long pause the clerk said, "Mrs. Robertson, let me be honest with you. We're running short of rooms tonight. We did not think you would be coming in, so we gave yours away. We've put you into a suite. There WAS a man in there, but we called up and told him to get in the bedroom and lock the door. I guess the cigar was his."

Then, before I could say anything else, he added, "But YOU'VE got the bathroom, and if it will make you feel any better, he just called down . . . and he's MORE AFRAID than you."

Warmly Delivered

One night in Boston, I called room service to order apple pie a'la mode. Right before I hung up, I double-checked, "The pie will be warmed up, won't it?"

"No, dear," the woman on the other end of the line answered, "We can't warm the pie if we put ice cream on top of it."

Now that just did not make sense to me. "Why not?" I asked.

I detected she did not think I was very smart. "BECAUSE, dear," she said with a false patience, "the ice cream will melt by the time it gets to your room." As with the bellman, this should have been a clue about how long it would take room service to get something to the room, but I did not pick up on it until later.

I persisted. "Can you give it a try?" It was my turn to fake patience. "In a lot of places I stay, if they put a scoop of cold ice cream on a piece of warm pie, it's JUST RIGHT when it gets to the room."

Long pause, then, "It will be a mess."

I tried again. "How 'bout if you put the ice cream in a little bowl and let me put it on the pie when it gets to the room?"

"Well, OF COURSE we can do that," she said condescendingly, "but you asked for it ON TOP OF the pie."

"Great, put it in a bowl." I answered. Knowing I could start getting ready for bed if a woman would be bringing the pie, I added, "And one more thing. Will a man or a woman be bringing the pie to the room?"

There was a very looong pause, and then she said curtly, "It will be brought up by a man, but NOTHING but the NICEST people work here. I can vouch for the man who will bring up the pie."

"Oh, that's not the problem," I quickly explained. "I wanted to go ahead and undress if by chance a woman would be bringing it up. But it doesn't matter."

"Well, you just go right ahead and undress. This is a VERY NICE MAN who has worked here for years. HE WILL NOT LOOK!"

A Matter of Opinion

We booked a Rotary Club Ladies Night in a small town which shall remain nameless. All of our dealings were with the vice-president of the club who was also the program chairman.

After we agreed on the fee, schedules, etc., this fellow asked if I minded staying in a private home; more specifically, with his wife and him. I told him that would be fine, and he went on to explain, "We've just got one little ol' motel here. It used to be pretty nice, but to tell you the truth, it was bought by some foreigners not long ago and it hasn't been the same. It's run-down and right dirty. Folks have sighted large rats in many of the rooms, and the new management is rude. I checked with the police chief who is a friend of mine and he agrees that you will not be safe there."

I assured him I would be happy to stay with his family. I did not care to room with rats in a place where I would not be safe.

About a month later, we received a call from the president of the club who told us the program chairman had moved away. This gentleman instructed us to send all correspondence to him from that point on. Just before we hung up, I asked, "Where will I be staying now?"

He said, "Oh, we've got one little motel here in town. I'll make a reservation for you."

Ayes Said Up

I was waiting for an elevator on the mezzanine of a high-rise hotel in Hollywood, Florida, when an absolutely gorgeous young woman walked up. We were exchanging pleasantries when one set of elevator doors opened. The elevator was packed with men of all ages and sizes, and although they were crowded, they began to make room for one more. I knew who the one more was, but I was inching my way in with her when someone said, "Going down?" We both stepped back quickly and said, "No, up." The doors shut and the elevator left.

A few seconds later, the doors opened to reveal the same packed group of men, each grinning from ear to ear. Their spokesman announced, "We voted, and decided to ride back up."

The Most Interesting Engagement?

"What's the most interesting speaking engagement you've ever had?" is the question people ask me second most often. (No question will ever outdistance, "How tall are you?") This is a difficult question to answer because there are no dull or routine speaking engagements. Groups of people just do not gather for anything without opening the possibilities that there will be unusual occurrences. As a matter of fact, by this stage of my career I know that I can rely on something unusual happening in every speaking situation.

Whether the event was carefully organized by the most experienced meeting planner, or thrown together by a bunch of good ol' boys who "ain't never planned nothin' like this before," I guarantee that in every speaking situation something humorous, if not downright unbelievable, will occur. Granted, it may not be seen by everyone. But if you look for humor, it is there. Quite frankly, I count on that being the case in order to gather material for future speeches and to continue to improve my own sense of humor by consciously looking for those happenings.

Years ago, at the conclusion of each speech I started writing down what made each speaking situation particularly memorable. A number of them immediately come to mind, such as:

. . . The luncheon when the center of the risers under the head table slowly collapsed, and all the dignitaries slid toward the middle.

. . . The seventy-fifth anniversary banquet when the officers of the company rolled in a huge cake with the appropriate number of candles . . . and the smoke got so thick, we had to evacuate the room.

. . . The time the banquet emcee announced, "The lovely centerpiece on each table is to be given away and here is how we will do it. Number off around the table, and whoever is #3 will get the centerpiece."

. . . The keynote speech in Mexico when the local taxi dispatcher's instructions came through the hotel sound system sporadically through my entire speech.

. . . The time the meeting planner asked if he could go ahead and introduce me and have the dessert served during my speech, and forgot what dessert he had ordered. Just when I had everything rollin', the lights went off, and a line of forty waiters and waitresses burst through the kitchen doors carrying flaming baked Alaskas over their heads, and dancing to the tune of "When the Saints Go Marching In."

. . . The time the company president in his annual remarks to his top management team, said, "I know I say things like this every year, but this year, I'm sincere."

. . . The August night in South Carolina when a bat flew into my dress while I was speaking and attached itself to the hem of my skirt.

. . . The morning I was speaking to several thousand people at a Tupperware Jubilee, and became aware that a man in the front row had on a T-shirt with the words, "No Sex! No Supper! Just TUPPER, TUPPER, TUPPER!"

. . . The banquet in Kentucky when they presented an award for perfect attendance . . . to a man who was not there.

. . . The time four televisions were set up around the room so the crowd could glance at a basketball game while they listened to me. "But we'll keep the sound down."

. . . The night the belly dancer came in for the company president's birthday, just as I got to my serious point. "I hate to interrupt you, honey, but I've got to get to another gig."

. . . The day I started my speech, received a cue to sit down when President Gerald Ford arrived to address the group for ten minutes (election year, of course); and resumed my program when he left.

. . . The time I spoke in Washington, D.C., over music piped through the P.A. system because the controls to the music were in the walk-in freezer, and the man with the key to the freezer locked it and left after he doled out the roast.

. . . The day in Montgomery, Alabama, when I gave my first humorous line, and everyone in the civic club picked up a dinner roll and threw it at me. It turned out that this is a long-standing custom in this club and means they like you and are glad you are there. I wish I had known that . . . because when several hundred rolls started flying through the air in my direction, I reacted by quickly picking up a plate of food and turning it over in the president's lap.

. . . The time I was emceeing a pageant and the curtain man just would not pick up on the cue to pull the curtain, so I went over and grabbed it as I started walking toward the center of the stage . . . and pulled the entire curtain off its track to the floor.

. . . The night in Orlando when the people in the kitchen got in a fight and were all sent home, and the hotel desk clerks and bellboys cooked the food.

. . . The Saturday night I was speaking at the Aircraft Owners and Pilots Association banquet at the close of a four-day convention, and right before I was introduced, a weatherman announced a bad front was moving into the area and the people in the audience would not be able to fly their planes out until at least Tuesday.

. . . The morning the man who was sent to the stage to introduce me announced that the company president died the night before, but would have wanted the meeting to go on. "And now, to remind us to keep a sense of humor . . . Jeanne Robertson."

. . . The night 350 farmers and their spouses lined up for a barbecue supper, and discovered there was not a plate, knife, or fork in the place—just lots of barbecue.

. . . The time a stray dog walked in the back door of an auditorium in Enterprise, Alabama, proceeded down the aisle, up the steps of the stage, and sat down next to me as I was speaking.

. . . The night I was emceeing a pageant, and the contestants dressed in evening gowns were being brought up from the basement on the movable orchestra pit for the grand opening. The pit got stuck halfway up and the girls had to climb out in front of a packed auditorium.

. . . The night two banquets were being held in adjacent rooms, and the kitchen staff served the $12.95 chicken plate to the people who paid $24.95 for steak, and vice versa. The steak people went into the next banquet room and tried to swap plates; and the chicken people, who were eating steaks by that time, would not swap.

. . . The time my client wanted to keep me a "secret" until I was introduced to speak. He instructed me not to go to the reception and to already be seated when guests came into the ballroom. "People might notice you if you're standing," he added.

At one point during the meal, I gathered my purse to freshen up in the ladies room. As I rose from the table, my contact grabbed my arm and said, "Would you mind squatting down a little when you walk out, so you won't draw attention?"

Picture that, please. There are several hundred people sitting at round tables at a banquet—carrying on casual banquet conversation—and a six-foot-two woman squatting to half her size comes sneaking by the tables. And the man did not want to draw attention?

. . . The banquet when the emcee began to hand out the plaques and at one point said, "Our top award this year goes to a man who set up the largest sales display in our company's history. Unfortunately, he's not here tonight. As you know, he passed away in . . . well, NOT LONG after setting up that big display."

. . . The sales meeting when the regional managers were introducing the sales reps and their spouses and one manager said, "From the southern region is Dave Jones." Dave began to stand, and the manager continued, "and his wife Susan." The woman was beginning to rise and she quickly corrected him. "Cheryl," she said, smiling sweetly. The introducer became flustered, but probably did not make things better when he said, "I'm sorry, Cheryl. Dave switches so often!"

. . . and, the convention where I had to speak in English, because it is all I know, to over three hundred people who spoke only Spanish. They thought Julio Iglesias was going to be the entertainment because the meeting planner HAD INSINUATED Julio Iglesias was going to be there. "I didn't EVER SAY Iglesias would be here," he protested, "I just didn't stop the rumor once it started flying."

These are just samplings of the many unusual speaking situations encountered since I started speaking to groups in 1963. The MOST INTERESTING speaking engagement I have ever had? Well, I always figure the most interesting speaking engagement . . . will be the one I have tomorrow, and I will be looking for the humor in it.

It's Your Turn to Work Magic

The humorous experiences presented in this chapter might cause you to ask several questions: Did the little old lady really pull out an airsick bag and fake an illness? Did the doctor on the van actually say, "Hundred thousand one . . . hundred thousand two?" Did the group of men on the elevator really vote to ride back up? The answer to all these questions is yes. All of the anecdotes presented in this chapter happened in my everyday experiences. I did not have to write them. I observed them because I was looking for them. Remember, if an individual is not aware anything humorous is happening around him, it does not mean that it is not occurring. More than likely, it means he just did not see it because he did not choose to look for it. You might be thinking that my everyday situations offer many more opportunities to find humor. Actually, humor is just a lifestyle and a way of looking at life. I sincerely believe that in any occupation or lifestyle you will find humor if you look at your everyday situations through humorous eyes.

To develop one's sense of humor, make it a priority to look for humor in everyday situations. So how do you get started? Here is my list of six key steps:

1. *Identify Your Daily Routine.* Try to determine the most likely places you will find humor. Basically, the opportunities to find humor are greater when you are with other people. The person who works at a computer from nine until five every day, will more than likely see humorous things during breaks, lunch, and as people gather in the morning or leave after work; whereas, a teacher will have continuous opportunities as the students come and go. Think about the people with whom you come in contact on a regular basis. Who are the most likely to say and do funny things? The most likely to share a humorous thought if they realize you would be receptive?

2. *Add Finding Humor to Your "To Do" List.* Right there along with "call the printer" and "go to the grocery store," scribble down "find something humorous in my everyday situations." Each time that you review your list will be a reminder to look for humor. Do not mark it off your list until you accomplish the task. When you do see something humorous, mark it off your list and jot down what you have found. Later transfer what you found or just drop your old "to do" list into a file which will grow into part of your personal humor collection.

3. *Ask Yourself Questions That Lead to Finding Humor.* "What is funny about that?" is an ideal question to ask when

viewing previously routine occurrences. "Is there a humorous side to what she just did?" "Will this be funny when I tell
it later?" If necessary, jot down one or all of these questions
at the top of your "to do" list until you develop the habit of
asking the questions without even thinking.

Asking leading questions to yourself is a great device to use
when you have to kill a little time standing in line or waiting
on a report. I have received more than a few quizzical glances
when I've been chuckling to myself after answering the question "What is funny about that?"

If you do not see a humorous side to a routine incident, say to
yourself, "Wouldn't it have been funny if . . ." and then let
your mind wander and exaggerate the situation. The mere
thought that something could have happened will bring a
smile to your face if not laughter.

> *A word of caution:* It is unwise to let your mind wander toward
> humor that is detrimental. What we think, we do indeed become
> because our overall thinking influences the way we act. It is a
> good policy to avoid thinking about ethnic jokes, religious or
> racial jokes or so-called cruelty jokes.

4. *Ask for Humor.* Rather than making idle chitchat with
   "Boy, it's gonna be hot today" or "How are the children?" say,
   "What's the funniest thing that has happened to you today?"
   or "Tell me something humorous."

At first people will greet you with blank stares. You may even
have to explain that you are looking for humor. They will
probably want to know why. Explain with a smile that you are
just trying to brighten your day.

Quite frankly, you will not receive mounds of humor at first,
but in the long run, this can be a valuable source of finding
humor in everyday situations. Your associates, friends, and
family will begin to see humorous happenings and report
them to you. When people know you place a high priority on
humor, they eagerly share stories with you.

When appropriate, I even ask strangers for humor—as I did with the cab driver in Spartanburg, South Carolina. In that case, I was told the incident about the hog. You cannot make up stuff like that. Ask and you will find it.

5. ***Work with a Humor Buddy.*** Once you make the decision to look for humor in everyday situations, tell someone you have made that a policy and later share what you find with them. Preferably, work with someone who is willing to do the same thing, and you will both reap the benefits. Be forthright. Explain that you need a humor buddy. You will find that others are as excited as you about the prospect of working on humor. Get in the habit of reporting to each other what you found that struck your funny bone. There will be days when you may have to say you forgot to find any humor. This only serves to increase your awareness in the future.

There is a second advantage to working with one or more humor buddies. By telling a humorous event you develop your ability to be funny. While being funny is not a prerequisite for having a delightful sense of humor, it is usually a talent that grows as one's sense of humor develops. Once you tell a funny story, you gain the confidence to repeat it to other people.

As a speaker, this is a marvelous practice. Not only does it assist me in collecting humor, but it also gives me opportunities to try out stories on a one-to-one basis before including them in a speech. "I've got one for you" and "Well, listen to what I saw" serve as a preface to hours of shared fun and great growth in everyone's sense of humor. I believe so strongly in this theory that I have several buddies with whom I eagerly share the humor I see, and vice versa.

6. ***Write It Down. Write It Down. Write It Down.*** You do not have to write out the humor you find, but do jot down enough to recall the incident. Drop it in your budding humor file.

Potion 3
Create Your Own Humor

A keen sense of humor is based on an ability to cut loose from our usual mode of thinking. It is being "in fun," and having the ability to be playful, even childlike, with that which is often thought to be serious. Such is frequently the case when we choose to create our own humor.

There are many occasions in which the atmosphere could be greatly improved with the injection of a little playfulness. It is precisely those times that the person dedicated to improving a sense of humor should take advantage of the opportunity. I am not referring to practical jokes that may hurt or embarrass others. I am referring to harmless, playful humor that results in fun for everyone. Well-planned, harmless practical jokes definitely have their place. However, it is best to determine the apparent

seriousness of the situation before being too playful, lest it back-
fire with consequences other than the intended pleasure.

In our daily routines we are confronted with two options in
most situations. One option is to take life very seriously and do
that which is expected. It is this predictable action that most
people choose to take. The second alternative is to let the little
child in us come out to play. Why not make life more exciting by
opting to be "in fun" and creating a little humor?

People who have a good sense of humor or have made the
decision to improve this realm of their personality are the ones
who initiate playfulness. Often this choice, to instigate a little
playfulness or to make a little humor, must be made in a split
second. On other occasions, it is worked out carefully in advance. Enjoy the following anecdotes which offer illustrations
of creating both impromptu humor and humor which requires
prior planning.

Proud Papa

A couple of days after I won the Miss North Carolina title, my
mother called me aside and said, "Jeanne, please don't stop being
the same person you were before you won. We like you the way
you are."

Good advice. Unfortunately she forgot to give it to
my father. When I became "Jeanne Swanner, Miss North
Carolina," Daddy became "Jim Swanner, FATHER OF Miss
North Carolina." If people came up and said, "Excuse me, but
aren't you Miss North Carolina?" Daddy would lean in and
brag, "She sure is, and I'm her father."

On one occasion, Daddy and I were riding in a crowded hotel
elevator. As we stared at the floor counter over the door, not a
soul said, "Aren't you Miss North Carolina?" I could see Daddy
looking around and I could read his mind. Daddy was surely
thinking, "Don't these people know who's on this elevator?"

By the time we got to the sixth floor, Daddy could not stand the anonymity any longer. He looked me right in the eyes and asked in a loud voice, "Say, aren't you Miss North Carolina?"

Daddy got the results he anticipated. The people on the elevator turned to look at me and started the usual comments. "Oh, you're the big one—from Graham." "You're the one who plays basketball." I thought, "and the one with the kooky father." I was smiling, of course, but while I answered their questions, my mind was racing. I thought, "Okay, Daddy, when we get off at the twelfth floor carrying identical luggage, all these people are going to say, 'There go two fools from Graham, North Carolina.'"

Daddy was ahead of me, and he was a person who knew how to create his own humor. When we got to the eleventh floor, he pushed the button and said in another loud voice, "Well, this is where I get off." To my amazement he reached over, picked up one of the suitcases, and walked off the elevator and down the hall. But before he left, as the elevator doors were closing, he turned and looked at me from head to toe, and in front of all those people he said, "I'll tell you one thing, honey. I bet you've got a good-looking daddy."

The Ulterior Motive

Many people really prefer the haughty-taughty, big hotels in large cities. I do not. Every time you turn around, someone has a palm turned up for a tip. I prefer the smaller places to stay . . . not much tipping and a lot funnier.

On one trip I checked into a small motel in Texas. The desk clerk said that someone would come to make up the room in a few minutes. When I got to the room, there were no linens—no sheets, pillows, towels, or blankets—just a bare mattress. My mind was preoccupied with business, and I sat down to make several long distance calls. In the middle of one conversation, there was a knock on the door. "I'm on long distance," I called out. "Just put the linens outside the door."

In a few seconds I became aware that someone had unlocked the door and tried to open it. The door came to an abrupt halt an inch and a half later. Out of habit I had put the chain lock in place.

Putting my hand over the receiver, I repeated, "I'm on long distance. Just leave the linens outside the door."

Before long I was distracted by more movement at the door. An unknown hand was carefully and methodically working a pillow through the small opening allowed by the chain. At first I tried to ignore what was going on, but as the pillow was being slowly crammed through the narrow opening, I gave up. "I'll have to call you back," I said. It is difficult to discuss business and laugh at the same time.

I walked over to the door, and let's be honest, all I had to do was unchain the door. But why? Much more fun to create a little humor. Without saying a word, I started pulling the pillow in from my side. I pulled and pulled, while the person on the other side pushed and pushed. In a few minutes the pillow popped into the room.

Then I looked down and saw the corner of one of those big, fluffy towels coming through the narrow space. Neither I nor the mysterious person on the other side of the door said a word. I just started pulling the towel through from my side. I was getting so tickled that I could barely pull, but I made myself continue as we slowly transferred all the linens, one by one, from the hall to the room. Finally, the last washcloth dropped through the opening.

By that time I was limp from laughter and sitting on the floor. Not a single word had been exchanged, and I was debating whether or not to open the door.

All of a sudden, an empty hand came quietly through the opening and around the edge of the door. When it was all the way inside, the hand suddenly flipped over, palm up . . . for a tip.

A Budding Rose

Through the years I have found it particularly enjoyable to work with high school-aged pageant contestants. They have usually never competed before, so it is all new to them and they get quite excited. They are fun to be around.

At one state pageant the sponsors gathered all the high school contestants on Sunday afternoon to explain the coming week's activities. As they talked, one of the pageant coordinators came in with a dozen long-stemmed roses in a vase. The director was handed the flowers, and she announced that they had been sent to one of the contestants. She asked, "Is anyone expecting flowers?" Most teenagers are not accustomed to receiving a dozen red roses, and the announcement generated excitement in the room.

While she fished for the card, no one spoke. Each, of course, was secretly hoping the roses were for her. Then the director walked over and handed them to one young woman, saying "They're for you."

The contestant's reaction was amazing. It was as though a pan of cold water had been dashed in her face. I had never seen anything like it. She was shocked . . . and thrilled! She threw her feet out in front of her, her arms went out to the side, and then she started jumping up and down. "I just can't believe it. Oh, I can't believe it. I've never gotten flowers in my life!"

Immediately the other contestants came rushing around her, and they were all jumping up and down with her. Naturally, they wanted to see who had sent the flowers. She pulled the card out of the envelope and looked at it. As the other contestants pressed forward to read the name of the sender, the young woman stepped back, and without saying a word, ate it. Put the card in her mouth, chewed it up, and ate it! Everybody stared at her in disbelief, and when she gave the final big swallow, they broke into cheers.

As the week progressed, all the girls got to know each other, but this girl—nicknamed "the flower child"—was the best known of all. They had seen her become so excited, and all week long they had kidded her about the incident. At every meal someone said, "Pass your leftovers to the flower child. She'll eat anything." While it soon became evident that she would not win the title, she was a shoo-in for the Miss Personality Award. Sure enough, on Saturday night she was elected Miss Personality, which meant that she was the most popular of all the contestants.

When the pageant was over, all the contestants' parents gathered on the stage, and I was introduced to Miss Personality's folks. I wanted them to know how much everyone liked their daughter and said, "I realize you may be disappointed that your daughter didn't win the title, but I want you to know how much she added to the excitement of the week." I told them about the roses. "Actually," I concluded, "your daughter's a character. Everybody loves her."

The mother looked at me for a few seconds as though debating whether to say something. Finally she smiled and said, "She's much more of a character than you will ever know. We own a floral shop. After our daughter left on Sunday morning, we discovered that she had wired a dozen red roses to herself, to be sent to pageant headquarters. She had to eat the card . . . it had her own name on it!"

The Total Woman

My sister Katherine and I were at a spouses' program during the Southeastern Propane Gas Association annual meeting in Atlanta. The speaker was a representative from Total Woman. There we sat—500 women from states like Georgia, South Carolina, and Alabama—listening to the speaker say, "Ladies, the time comes in every marriage when you need to spice it up just a little." My sister whispered, "I told you this would be better than the tour of Stone Mountain."

"For example," the speaker continued, "one afternoon before your spouse gets home from work, take off all your clothes (right there I would have to start around two o'clock) and cover your body in . . . Saran Wrap, and maybe some mayonnaise. You'll really surprise him." (Katherine surprised me with an elbow in the ribs.)

My mind wandered to a mental picture of Jerry coming home late one afternoon, dead tired. As he opened the door, he would find me covered in Saran Wrap and mayonnaise. I could not help but see another picture. Just how much mayonnaise do you think it would take to cover a 6'2" body? I live in a small town. Word would spread as soon as I checked out of the grocery store with seventeen quarts of mayonnaise.

All the women in the audience listened intently, but that night at the banquet several of them were making fun of the mayonnaise and Saran Wrap bit. One woman, though, spoke in defense of the idea. "Wait a minute," she said. "I'm not the mayonnaise and Saran Wrap type either, but the speaker had a point. Every relationship does need a little shocker now and then. I don't know what my little shocker will be," she continued, "but I'll know it when I see it." Apparently, she saw it the following Halloween.

At the next year's annual convention, this lady could not wait to find me and tell me of her little shocker, which she swore was true.

All of her children were out trick or treating and her husband was sitting in the den, reading the paper. Very quietly she tiptoed upstairs to the bedroom. Taking off all her clothes, she put on her raincoat and crept back down the stairs to the kitchen where she pulled out a big, brown grocery sack. Then she went around the house in the dark to the front porch, slipped the bag over her head, and rang the doorbell.

Her husband put down the paper and went to open the front door. As he stood there, she stepped forward—bag still over her head—and flung her raincoat open. "Trick or treat!"

How much trouble do you think a man is in when he looks right at his wife's body and says, "Who is it?"

The Thanksgiving Switch

I inherited my dislike for cooking quite honestly. My Grandma Freddie HATED cooking, but she did like to entertain. Even though she was tight with her money, she believed that as matriarch of the clan she should host the large family holiday dinners. Family members will never forget one particular Thanksgiving when my aunt and uncle decided to create a little humor.

Everyone was gathered at the matriarch's home on College Street in Auburn, Alabama, for the traditional turkey dinner. While Grandma Freddie and most of the family socialized in the living room and on the porch, my Uncle Lan and Aunt Carolyn sneaked into the house through the kitchen door. They had a small Cornish hen that they had browned and cooked, just as one would cook a turkey. It looked for all the world just like a miniature gobbler.

They opened the oven door and slowly and carefully lifted out the twenty-five pound turkey Grandma Freddie had cooked for dinner. They substituted the Cornish hen and hid the real thing outside on the carport.

After a while, Grandma Freddie came to the kitchen to check on the turkey that she was to feed to 28 hungry people. Family members, who were all in on the humor with the exception of the small "can't keep a secret children," casually followed her to the stove or hung around outside the kitchen to hear the reaction.

She opened the oven door and peered in. "Good Lord!" she screamed, and then added in disgust as she slammed the hot pad down on the counter, "THAT'S what I get for buying a CHEAP turkey. IT SHRUNK!"

The Saturday Night Miracle

My Aunt Carolyn loves to tell about a personal friend of hers in South Carolina, an older doctor whose son had gone into practice with him. Their office was a side room on the senior doctor's house.

Like most towns, this one had a couple of rough spots where local rowdies gathered on Friday and Saturday night to celebrate the advent of the weekend. The evenings frequently ended in brawls, after which friends loaded buddies in need of repair into their automobiles and headed to the doctor's house. Naturally, the same people showed up over and over during the course of time.

One particular Saturday night, the older doctor looked out his window and saw a long caravan of cars winding slowly down the street. It seemed that for no reasonable explanation, in the middle of a dance, one of the locals collapsed unconscious on the floor. Most of revelers at the club accompanied the people who carried the unconscious soul to seek medical assistance, and they all crowded into the doctor's small office. They thought the fellow was dead, and they were particularly interested because many of them had drunk the same stuff. Actually, he was a severe diabetic and had lapsed into a coma from lack of insulin—a fact the doctor knew from having treated him many times.

The physician quickly injected the patient with what he knew would revive him as soon as it got into the bloodstream. As he waited for the medicine to take effect, the doctor looked around the room at all the wide and slightly blurred eyes staring first at him and then to the body on the table. Taking into account the amount of time needed for the medicine to work, he proceeded to create a little humor. The doctor put his hands over the patient and started chanting, "Do you hear me, brother John? John. OOOOOOh, Johnnnnnn. On the count of ten, arise and join your brethren. One, two, three . . . ."

On the count of ten, brother John slowly opened his eyes and started moving. The eyes all around the room got bigger and BIGGER, and in just a matter of minutes, the caravan of cars carried a group of very subdued people—several of whom had been born again—up the street with brother John sitting in a front seat.

The next day, a patient came to the office and the receptionist started to mark her down to see the younger doctor. "No," she said. "I want to see the one what brings 'em back from the dead."

For years after that, every time the older doctor drove through town, mothers brought their children out to wave at him.

A New Product

Of course, the creation of humor can be carried a little too far. I believe my grandfather might have gone to extremes when he decided to have a little fun years ago. The story is now legend in the small town of Auburn, Alabama.

My Grandma Freddie was to hostess the monthly afternoon meeting of the women of the First Methodist Church in Auburn. She had refreshments, of course, but right before the ladies arrived, my grandfather brought in several boxes of a new chewing gum from his drugstore for the ladies. She did not recognize the brand, but assumed it was just another new gum left by a salesman. She was correct. It was a new product in the form of chewing gum . . . called Feen-a-mint.

As the ladies arrived for the long afternoon meeting, Grandma Freddie greeted each with a small box of the new gum. It tasted good; so good, in fact, that many of them spent the afternoon putting pieces in their mouth as soon as the flavor waned on the previous piece. By three-thirty that afternoon, ladies were lined all the way down the hall outside Grandma Freddie's bathroom.

My grandfather later introduced the product to customers at the drugstore saying, "Tested, and the seal of approval given, by the United Methodist Women of Auburn, Alabama."

Worthy Recipient

I flew into one city that shall remain nameless, took a cab to the hotel, and slept all afternoon. That night I spoke at the city's annual chamber of commerce banquet held in that same facility. I never left the hotel.

When I finished my speech, the president of the chamber called me back to the lectern and presented me with a plaque for my "Outstanding Contributions to the City." That amused me since I had been in the city less than eight hours and had not left the hotel, but I accepted the plaque in the seriousness with which it was given, had my picture made, and sat down. I gave up trying to figure out "outstanding contributions" and plaques a long time ago. I thought I had given a pretty good speech, but an "outstanding contribution to the city?" Hardly. On this particular occasion, it was a beautiful wooden plaque, but my name was not even on it. I call them generic plaques.

The next morning I took a cab to the airport. My driver had been "born and raised," as he put it, in this city and had been driving a cab there for over thirty years. He was a neat old fellow and seemed to really enjoy telling me all about his town.

I do not know what made me do what I did. I certainly did not plan it. When we pulled up to the curb at the airport, I unzipped my hanging bag and pulled out the plaque. After I paid the driver and we were standing on the sidewalk, I said, "Paul, I'm a representative of the chamber of commerce. Over the years, numerous people have told us how well you represent the city to people who fly in and out of this airport. Not only that, it has come to our attention that you genuinely care about the people who live here and that you always have a friendly smile for your passengers. Therefore, on behalf of the chamber, I am proud to present you this plaque for 'Outstanding Contributions to the City.' Keep up the good work." With that said, I handed him the plaque, shook his hand, and left a dumbfounded, old cab driver standing on the sidewalk . . . with tears in his eyes.

I felt so good about what I had done that when I found myself in a similar situation a few weeks later in Chicago, I changed my words a little and gave a framed Certificate of Appreciation I had just received to a cabby driving me to O'Hare. It turned out he appreciated plaques and certificates about as much as I do. He read the certificate, cut his eyes up at me and said, "Do a check come with it?"

Bewildered and Thirsty

A man boarded the flight when I did in Edmonton, Alberta, Canada. We were to fly to Calgary, then on to Dallas. After he settled in, he found the flight attendant. Without even so much of a hint of insincerity, he said that he needed to tell her about something that would happen in a little while when the plane landed in Calgary.

Very seriously he described a passenger who would board the flight in Calgary and added, "The first thing he'll probably do is order a Chevis Regal Scotch, and you've got to be careful about giving it to him." The flight attendant listened intently. He went on to say that the man he described was on the "Addicted Imbibing List" with the Alberta Province of Canada. "This means he is not allowed to drink on the ground in the Province. Therefore, he goes crazy when he gets on a flight and can drink."

She bought it, and nodded her head. "I understand."

"Just thought you ought to know," this fellow added, "so you could handle any situation that might arise. It could be bad."

I had been carefully eavesdropping on the entire conversation and had to fight to keep from laughing. It was evident someone was being set up—"Addicted Imbibing List," indeed.

We arrived in Calgary, and sure enough, the passenger who had been described boarded the flight and greeted his friend before taking a seat in the next row. As he stored his carry on luggage, the flight attendant looked at the friend who nodded at her as if to say, "that's the one."

This unsuspecting soul settled in his seat and promptly placed his order. "Scotch and water, Chevis if you have it," he said with a smile. But the flight attendant had given this situation careful thought during the flight from Edmonton to Calgary.

"I'm sorry, sir. I think it would be best for you to stick with a soft drink." His buddy had to look out the window to keep from laughing.

"A soft drink? No way. If you do not have Chevis, I'll take any Scotch."

"Sir," she said, lowering her voice and tucking her chin. "I KNOW about the list."

When she said that, the friend who had set up this little practical joke sprayed the swallow he had just taken all over the seat in front of him.

"The what?" the unsuspecting passenger asked.

She leaned in closer. "We BOTH KNOW you are on the Addicted Imbibing List, and I believe it will be best if you have a soft drink."

The fellow was bewildered, but not as bewildered as I when he slid down in his seat like a hurt puppy and said, "I'll have a ginger ale."

Questionable Identification

I was standing sideways in the aisle waiting to deplane in Dallas, Texas, when I became aware of a gentleman staring at me. He was a short, hefty fellow wearing a big cowboy hat and chewing on a toothpick. I nodded, and he nodded back and continued to stare.

I looked everywhere I could, but my eyes finally rested on him again. He was still just "a chewing" on his toothpick and looking right at me. I smiled a second time. He nodded again and kept staring. Suddenly, he took the toothpick out of his mouth, nodded toward my ukulele, and inquired, "You play that thing?"

"Yes," I answered.

He put the toothpick back in his mouth and continued to stare. His brow wrinkled. I could tell he had slipped his thinking into overdrive. After a few minutes he reached up, took his tooth-pick out again, and said, "Are you one of them Mandrell sisters?"

I smiled and shook my head. "No."

He tilted his head back, squinted his eyes at me for a few seconds, leaned in my direction, and said, "Yes you are."

I leaned toward him and looked right into his eyes. "No I'm not."

He began to grin and shook the toothpick at me before saying again, even more emphatically, "YES YOU ARE."

Shaking my head back and forth, I glanced around as though I did not want the other passengers to hear what he was saying, put my finger to my lips and said, "Shsss."

He smiled, nodded his head up and down and mouthed, "I won't tell anybody."

I mouthed, "Thank you."

We got off the plane and as I walked toward the terminal, I just happened to look back. He was staring at me again, but this time he winked and waved goodbye.

I waved back and then thought, "What the heck? Why not make a little more humor?" Taking out a piece of paper, I wrote, "Love ya." At the baggage claim, I slipped the paper into his hand.

I got in a cab and started laughing. The next time one of the Mandrell sisters is on television, I could visualize him shaking his head and telling his family, "No, it wasn't that one. It was the TALL sister."

The last picture ever made of Jeanne Robertson with her mouth closed.

Jeanne whips out her baritone ukulele during certain speeches, ignoring the time someone said, "See how little that guitar looks next to her *Biggggg* body."

At six-feet-two inches tall, Jeanne had to bend at the knees to be crowned Miss North Carolina. Perhaps the microphone in front of her was an omen of a professional speaking career.

Parents Jim and Cora Swanner, and sisters Katherine S. Mussell and Andrea Swanner, gather around after Jeanne was crowned Miss North Carolina. Notice only one member of the family has her mouth open.

Most folks thought Jeanne presented comedy for her talent in the Miss America Pageant. Not true. She sang and played the ukulele the best she could. People just *thought* it was comedy.

Jeanne jokingly says, "The Miss Congeniality Award goes to the contestant whom the others believe is the least likely to win the title of Miss America." In reality, she cherishes the title given her by the other state winners.

Jeanne fights to keep the basketball away from her son Beaver, left, and husband Jerry. What else would a tall family do in their spare time?

Women's Olympic basketball coach Kay Yow presents an autographed ball to Jeanne after her speech to the 1988 Olympic team. Jeanne told the players, "I wanted to shoot hook shots for my talent in the Miss America Pageant, but officials would not let me. I think they were afraid I might win. The headlines would have read, 'Hooker Wins Miss America!'"

Two humorous speakers fight over one microphone at a banquet in Raleigh, NC. Jeanne says, "This rare sought-after photo of Coach Jim Valvano unable to speak is worth the price of this book."

Jeanne Robertson with her older brother, father, and grandfather.

O.K., O.K. So they're not relatives. But they are Jeanne's associates in
Platform Professionals. They are (L to R) humorists Robert Henry, Joe
Griffith, and Doc Blakely. They coauthored the book "How The
Platform Professionals *Keep 'Em Laughin'*," published by Rich Publish-
ing Company.

Once you have been in the Miss America Pageant, you never forget how to smile.

"Don't laugh 'til I give you the punch line," Jeanne tells a fellow at the Kentucky Municipal League Convention.

Jeanne gets handcuffed and led away by a police officer at the end of a program in her hometown. Was the speech that bad? No. It was all part of her role as Honorary State Chairman of the North Carolina Cancer Crusade. She was set free when her friends raised the appropriate amount of "bail." It took a while.

Jeanne can't help but clown a little while serving as TV hostess during PBS Festival Week in North Carolina.

Jeanne loves to turn the tables on men with her hilarious "There He is ... Mr. Convention" audience participation.

The group's reaction tells it all as Jeanne uses audience participation to illustrate a point.

He who laughs last laughs loudest!

There's always one . . .

It's too bad Jeanne doesn't seem to enjoy her work!

The payoff. Jeanne congratulates the winner in this contest, "Mr. Pembroke State University."

Nido Qubein, CPAE, one of the nation's leading speakers and then President of the National Speakers Association, presents Jeanne with the President's Award for Distinguished Service.

Arnold "Nick" Carter, CPAE, presents Jeanne with the CPAE Award, the highest award given by the National Speakers Association for excellence in speaking. One of the other three recipients that year was President Ronald Reagan.

Jeanne is a funny woman, but her peers saluted her business sense when they elected her President of the National Speakers Association.

The highest honor the National Speakers Association bestows on one of its members is the Cavett Award. "The Cavett" recognizes the professional speaker who has done the most to bring honor and prestige to the world of professional speaking and the over 3,000 members of NSA. In 1989, Jeanne became the eleventh speaker and the first woman to receive the award.

A Cookin' Cat

Leaving Indianapolis on a flight to Atlanta, a group of four people boarded the plane and sat near me. They were on their way to a convention where one of them would give some type of presentation that involved the use of a microwave oven. They had a small oven with them, and delighted in telling passengers that they had a cat in a special little traveling box. "It prevents air sickness," one of them explained, and burst out laughing.

They had all types of one liners like, "You would have somewhere to put your feet if you had not brought the cat." And as the flight attendants served lunch they asked, "Do you have any tuna?" and "Can you put that in a saucer?" It was evident to everyone they had already had too much to drink from their "saucers."

The plane made a stop in Nashville which brought, "I'd have taken another flight if I had known there was a stopover. The cat does not like to go up and down." Every comment built on the previous one and threw them into hysterics. Of course, one of them would then say, "Shsss, the cat's asleep," and they would burst out laughing again.

They were having a ball and it was funny, but the crowning remark came as we were leaving. They had gathered the microwave oven, handling it very carefully so as "not to disturb the cat." "She's sleeping," one of them added. The flight attendant—who had been a terrific sport through the entire thing—smiled and said, "Could you people POSSIBLY have stopped by the bar before this flight?" The man carrying the oven pulled himself to a haughty position and said, "I'll have you know madam, THIS CAT DOES NOT DRINK!"

Easily Recognized

Before each speech, we send the client an information sheet that outlines the details of my travel. If the client checks that someone will meet my plane, the next question is, "How will Jeanne recognize this individual?"

One group of secretaries answered, "Bill, a little middle-aged and normally a very distinguished-looking gentleman, will be waiting for Jeanne at the terminal entrance. He will be wearing a clown's outfit and carrying a purple sign with white lettering that reads 'Welcome Jeanne.' If there is more than one person at the terminal who fits this description, Jeanne should GET BACK ON THE PLANE AND GO HOME! WE WILL HAVE ALL GONE NUTS!"

Mistaken Identity

On Friday, January 30, 1981, I was to meet my husband Jerry at the Miami airport after a speaking engagement. We were going on a cruise with professional speakers from the National Speakers Association. I was coming from Mt. Pleasant, Texas, and Jerry was coming from home. I was scheduled to arrive in Miami a couple of hours before he was to arrive, so I decided to have a little fun.

I made a couple of small "I love you, Jerry" signs and put them up in the gate area. Then I bought several balloons and had "I love you" and "Welcome" written on them, and tied them around the door that leads from the gate where his plane was to dock. People watched me make all these preparations and began to stand around to see this special person come off the plane. When I finished my task, I chuckled to myself, stood back across the hall, and waited.

As the plane taxied up to the gate, a woman approached me and introduced herself. I thought she seemed particularly solemn, but I did not put two and two together. She patted me on the arm and said, "I know what you've been going through. Our thoughts and prayers have been with you the entire time." I did not know what she was talking about, and then she called attention to the small yellow ribbon pinned to her blouse. "I've worn this yellow ribbon for the past several days, but I didn't dream I'd get to welcome one of the hostages home in person." My mind raced, and it dawned on me! She thought I was to greet one of the Iranian hostages. They had been released that week. "No," I began. "I'm meeting my husband here. We're going on a cruise and. . . "

"And WELL YOU SHOULD, dear. Well you should. YOU DESERVE a little time together."

At that moment, the jetway door opened. I started to explain the true situation to the woman, but stopped. What the heck? I walked with her and joined the small crowd that had gathered. In a few seconds conservative, quiet Jerry Robertson walked through the door, and everyone broke into thunderous applause.

It is a good thing he doesn't mind when I create a little humor.

Designer Labels

We never pushed our son Beaver into basketball . . . much. We just said, "If you want to eat, you play." Basketball runs rampart in North Carolina, and we are certainly fans of the sport. It rubbed off on him as it does on many young people. From an early age he wanted to play.

One summer in the late seventies he went to four basketball camps. The coaches at one of the camps had the nerve to write me a pre-camp letter that read, "Mrs. Robertson, When you bring your son to our camp, please do not mark his name in his clothes with a black laundry marker. We PREFER that you hand sew in labels with his name."

Ha! Hand sew in labels? Sure. I thought it was a joke letter and when I realized it was not, I put it on the floor and kicked it. I created a little humor when I wrote them back.

"My name is Jeanne Robertson. I will be at camp with my son on July 13th. His name is . . . Levi Izod."

Doleful Initiation

I went to the lavatory to freshen my make-up midway through a long flight from Portland, Oregon, to Dallas. As I stood at the small mirror, my purse fell over and all my cosmetics fell into what is politely called a "water closet," but what I would refer to as a commode. Anyway, there is no water in an airplane water closet, so I carefully began to pick the items out, one by one. I had to tread lightly because the flap in the bottom had opened slightly under the weight of the cosmetics. Before I could rescue many of the little containers, the majority of them slipped through the opening. I groped as fast as I could, but to no avail. They were gone.

With the way I think, I quite naturally thought that it was humorous that over half of my cosmetics disappeared so quickly in such a place. When I walked past the plane kitchenette, I told the flight attendant what had happened. It gave her an idea about creating a little humor.

A few minutes later she came back and asked if I would help the crew with a little practical joke. It seemed the flight engineer was on his inaugural flight, and the crew had been looking for a way to make his first trip memorable. They wanted me to tell him I had dropped something valuable into the commode, and then try to persuade him to look for it. She asked if I thought I could handle it. (Does a fifty pound sack of flour make a BIIIGGGG biscuit?)

She soon returned to my seat with the "pigeon." I would be less than honest if I did not modestly admit I should have received some sort of Academy Award for my performance from that point on. I acted as though I was very upset because I had dropped my Rolex watch—studded with diamonds—down the commode. In reality, I had dropped my six-year-old Timex in my purse before he arrived at my seat. He was very polite as he explained that everything went into a big container and that when we arrived in Dallas, someone with the airline could get the watch for me.

I fabricated some tears, and then said I had a close connection in Dallas and could not wait. "Couldn't you just look for it now?" I wanted to know. He ignored my question and said that they would call ahead and have people waiting.

More tears. I wanted to know who was flying the plane at that exact time, and he patiently explained that the pilot and copilot were in charge. "Well, then," I said, "as long as YOU are not DOING anything, why can't you look?" Now remember, this man was on his first flight. He wanted to impress his associates and he certainly wanted to avoid any problems, and here was this crying woman. . . . He looked at the flight attendant. She shrugged her shoulders and contributed by saying, "We've got a plastic bag you could wear over your hand and arm if you want to take a look."

"OK," he sighed. "I'll see what I can do."

The flight attendant produced the plastic sack and into the lavatory he went. He got down on his hands and knees and reached as far as he could through the opening. He reached and groped and reached and groped, but it was the strangest thing. All he could find . . . were a few cosmetics.

When he gave up, the flight attendants and crew burst into applause, and he knew he had been inaugurated.

Later, the flight attendant brought me an unopened bottle of champagne, compliments of the Captain.

Creative Picture

High schools traditionally have one location where the photographers make all group pictures for the yearbooks. At my high school, the location was on the bleachers in the gymnasium. Year after year the club members could be seen in the annual lined up on the pulled-out bleachers. At other schools, it could be the auditorium, the school lawn, or as in the case of my son's high school in Burlington, the steps that lead up to the main entrance of the building.

Beaver and a lot of his friends were in the Civitan Club. Unfortunately, they were all going through their animal stages at the same time, and civic club work did not fit into their agendas. It is difficult to describe how inactive this group of guys was, but maybe I can give you an idea and at the same time illustrate someone's initiative in creating a little humor.

Of course, all of the inactive club members showed up the day pictures were taken for the annual; and when the yearbook came out, it contained pictures of all the other clubs with the respective members lined up on the traditional steps. Under each picture was an appropriate leadership-type caption such as: "Civinettes: Service is our Bottom Line" or "Keywanettes are Flying High." The Civitan Club's picture also had a caption: "Civitans: Always Around When you Need 'Em." And the picture was of the school steps . . . without a person standing there.

Rewards of Brevity

I was in Biloxi, Mississippi, waiting to speak at a company sales meeting. The company president was absent and a vice president was introduced to fill the spot.

The substitute strode to the stage, carrying a thick stack of pages of prepared text from the president. He took several moments to spread the speech out on the lectern, get the microphone adjusted, and clear his throat. People shifted positions in their seats and rolled their eyes at each other while they waited for him to begin. Finally, he did.

"I've been trying to tell J.N. to shorten his speech for the last three meetings. I didn't know I would have the chance to do it for him." With that he ripped the papers into little pieces, threw them into the air, and sat down.

There was thunderous applause.

Registration Surprise

When I checked into a hotel in Winnipeg, Manitoba, Canada, the desk clerks could not wait to share a story with me. It was about a gentleman who traveled for his company and stayed overnight at that hotel every month. He was the jovial, kidding type who enjoyed creating humor, so naturally the hotel and restaurant personnel knew and liked him.

During one trip he changed his standard reservation for the following month from a single to a double and commented in doing so that his wife would be accompanying him on the next trip. It seemed they would be leaving on a vacation after his business meeting. The hotel staff lay in wait for him.

A month later, when the man and his wife walked into the lobby, the clerk at the desk reached under the counter and pulled out a woman's hair dryer. "We're so glad to have you back again," she said. "Your wife left her hair dryer last month and we've been keeping it for you."

Blessed Event

I take an extra copy of my typed introduction with me to every speech. It is on a regular 8″ × 11″ piece of paper, folded letter style. I keep it in my travel packet with a copy of my birth certificate, also folded like a letter, and other travel documents. It is not unusual for an introducer to misplace the intro, and when that happens, I just whip out my copy.

Because of one particular incident, I am now verrrry careful to double-check which piece of paper I give the introducer. You become careful about such things once you make the mistake of handing the introducer your birth certificate rather than the speech introduction. I remember saying something like, "Just read it like it's written." Most people would have opened the paper, seen the error, and called it to my attention. However, this gentleman was a man who enjoyed creating a little humor. He realized what must have happened . . . but decided to play it to the hilt. What ensued was priceless.

He began. "Our speaker tonight was born in Chelsea, Massachusetts, on September 21, 1943." You can imagine my reaction. Shock must have registered all over my face because the audience reacted by bursting into laughter.

"My birth certificate!" I shouted. "You've got the wrong thing!" I stood up at the head table to go toward the lectern, but this guy was a gem. He pulled the paper back away from my reach, put his hand out to stop me, and said, "I know you reached in your purse and gave me the wrong paper. This is your birth certificate, but you said to read it as it's written, and I'm going to do just that. Now sit down!"

The audience just broke up. It was wonderful and this fellow knew it.

He continued, "Her mother was listed as Cora Lipscomb Swanner. Her father was . . . (long pause) . . . unknown." There were shrieks of laughter and people pounded their fist on the tables.

He continued, "She weighed 16½ pounds and was 28 inches long. Her footprints took up the entire paper! Ladies and gentlemen, our speaker for the evening, Jeanne Robertson."

When I reached the lectern, I stood there a few seconds as the laughter continued. Then, apparently perplexed, I turned to this gentleman and questioned, "Did you say I was born in '43? Let me see that thing!" He handed me the certificate. I stood at the microphone for a few more seconds, looking at the birth certificate, apparently deep in thought and pretending to count on my fingers. The audience waited silently. I finally looked up in anguish and said, "I'm a year older than I thought."

(For the record, my father was James Cleveland Swanner, Jr. AS LISTED on my birth certificate.)

Artful Joker

Although I concentrate on creating impromptu humor, I have been known to pull a few elaborate practical jokes over the years. Perhaps one of the best practical jokes I ever pulled was on a good friend of mine and fellow speaker buddy, Robert Henry. It happened during an annual convention of the National Speakers Association.

This particular annual convention was held in Scottsdale, Arizona. Over a thousand professional speakers were expected to gather for the four-day event, but the board of directors came in early for two days of meetings. I was serving as national president of NSA that year and Robert, as a past president, was in attendance as an ex officio member of the board.

Robert also came in early for the meeting for another reason. He was especially excited about the convention that summer because he was to be the keynote speaker during the opening luncheon on Sunday. It was to be a grand occasion for him . . . keynoting a convention of his peers . . . and it was a speech that he had carefully prepared for two years. When I realized I would be moving up the chairs into the presidency, I knew I wanted humorist Robert Henry to open "my" convention. When I appointed Ed Kelsay from Oklahoma as convention chairman, one of my main requests of him was to make sure to kickoff the convention with the funny man from Auburn, Alabama. Ed agreed.

When I was in the process of setting up my practical joke on Robert, I knew I needed help to give it credibility. Ed agreed to help me, and so did the president-elect, Dr. Jim Tunney. You might have seen Jim on television. He is an NFL referee, and can seem so serious that I thought he would be believable. I surmised

Robert would be suspicious of Ed and me, but not of Jim. I explained my idea to Ed and Jim, and they laughed so much that I became concerned they would not be able to get through their part in my scheme without breaking up. They did not let me down.

On the first day of the board meeting, Ed came in to report on the convention and put the plan into action. As he concluded his remarks, he said in front of everyone, "Jeanne, do you want me to tell them about the possible big surprise?" The twenty board members shifted their eyes toward me.

"No, not at this time. Let's get a little more information about it." He nodded in agreement.

"But maybe," I continued, "you should talk to Robert about it now." Turning toward an unsuspecting Robert I said, "Would you step outside with Ed for a few minutes? He needs to brief you about something that has come up for the convention." To my president-elect I said, "Jim, please step out with them since you are aware of this situation."

A hush fell over the room as Ed, Jim, and an unsuspecting Robert walked out into the hall. All I could think of was, "Don't let Jim and Ed get tickled."

When the door shut behind them, I let the board in on what we were doing. Right at that moment, Ed and Jim were informing Robert that President Ronald Reagan might be coming to the convention, and if he did come, he would be presenting a speech at the Sunday luncheon—Robert's slot! I knew that Robert would believe this story for several reasons: (1) NSA had presented President Reagan with its CPAE Award in 1981; (2) we thought we almost had him speak at our 1983 convention; and (3) Nancy Reagan's family lived in the Phoenix area. The board loved it and agreed not to let Robert know the truth: that President Reagan was not—and never had been—coming to our convention that year. Robert did not know that. All he heard out in the hall was that he might not get to give his speech

Sunday, a speech he had worked on for so long and was emotionally prepared to give. His children had come to the convention to hear him. He was not happy.

They tell me Robert acted like a pro when he heard the news. First he asked if there could possibly be any other time the President could be on the program. When Ed and Jim indicated there was not, he simply beat his head against the wall, dropped to his knees, and begged.

Ed and Jim assured Robert that it was not definite Reagan would be coming and they would tell him as soon as they found out. All three returned to the board meeting.

By the time they came back into the room, we had moved to another agenda item. No one even looked Robert's way. At the next break, I pulled Robert off to the side and told him I was sorry. He let down a little with me. "I just can't believe it," he kept saying. "I can't believe the President wants MY luncheon slot. The man could speak anywhere in the world. Why here? Why Sunday lunch?"

"It's not definite," I kept saying, "but Robert, you might as well know that it looks pretty solid." He started shaking his head. I continued, "But I promise you this, I'll strongly recommend to next year's convention chairman that you be considered to speak."

The day went on . . . and so did the practical joke. During the afternoon break, I told Robert that we had had another call from the White House and it looked as though Reagan would be coming. "Nancy's folks live in Phoenix," I reminded him. "They want an excuse to come this way." Robert's face fell, but by then he was saying things like, "Well, it will be mighty good for the Association, mighty good." He was trying to convince himself.

At the conclusion of the board meeting, there is a dinner for the directors and their spouses. At this evening event we stand up and tell stories about each other. Since we are all professional speakers with an array of war stories, you are correct to imagine it is a very funny evening. At the beginning of the dinner that night, I again called Robert over to the side and broke the news to him. It was confirmed. President Reagan would be speaking during the Sunday luncheon. "But, how about this," I said, putting my hand on Robert's shoulder. "Even though I'm President of NSA, I want you to introduce President Reagan for his speech."

"Oh, no," Robert said, with faked pitifulness. "That's your right."

"No, Robert. I want you to do it. There will be a lot of media people here. It will make all the networks. I want you to have the opportunity since you are giving up your speaking slot."

He cut his eyes at me. "It is the least you can do," he said and broke into a grin. "OK, I'll introduce him."

The board dinner continued for several hours. I later found out that during the entire meal, Robert and his wife Merrilyn sat at their table working on the introduction. After all, it is not every day one introduces the President of the United States. When the evening drew to a close, I got everyone's attention one last time. My husband thought it was time to put Robert out of his misery. I wanted to let it go one more day, but Jerry was right. Anyway, since the entire board had gone along with it, everyone should be there at the finale.

Calling Robert to the front, I began to recount all of the things he had done to me over the years. Lest you begin to feel sorry for him or think me cruel in any way, let me just say that this practical joke in NO WAY made us even.

I could tell Robert didn't know what on earth I was leading up to. " . . . and therefore, Robert, just to pay you back a little for all the things you've done to me through the years, I want to tell you that President Reagan is NOT coming Sunday and he NEVER HAS BEEN COMING."

It was as though he lost his summer tan in three seconds. His face drained to a very pale white as he registered shock and utter disbelief, and then we all burst out laughing. And we laughed 'til it hurt.

As of this day, Robert Henry still has not evened the score for this little episode. But on cold, dark nights, his words from that evening still ring in my ears. "Robertson, I'm gonna get you. Someday, somewhere, when you least expect it . . . without a clue . . . ."

Actually, if you think about it, I gave Robert a clue that we were pulling a practical joke. As president of the association and with the media buzzing around, there was NO WAY I would have given up introducing the President of the United States.

Robert just did not think . . . .

It's Your Turn to Work Magic

Now it is your turn to create a little humor which is either impromptu or carefully planned in advance. Many opportunities to create impromptu humor will be present if you make humor a significant element of your lifestyle. At first, proceed with caution and let the child in you come out to play only in situations where you feel most comfortable. You do not want your actions to result in embarrassment or bad feelings. Successful efforts initially will result in more frequent attempts and fun for everyone.

On other occasions, plan your humor carefully in advance. As suggested by the many examples in this chapter, the use of harmless practical jokes is a good technique that can easily be employed with a little forethought. Begin by devising a few simple practical jokes with your family and friends. Make these jokes simple so that you can anticipate with certainty that the intended results will be pleasurable. Efforts at planning and implementing harmless practical jokes will enhance your sense of humor.

Potion 4
Associate with People Who Have a Sense of Humor

O ne of the most successful ways to develop humor as a life-style is to associate with people who have a sense of humor. Notice I did not say associate with comedians or people who always fancy themselves as the life of any gathering. While it is enjoyable to be around funny people, quite often the funniest types may not be so hilarious when under stress. Associating with humorous people implies a relationship with individuals who, like you, understand the magic of humor and the importance it can play in a person's lifestyle. I am not referring to the casual bystander, the clerk in the store, or the hotel bellman—people we see fleetingly as we go about our lives. Rather, I am referring to the individuals in our immediate circles, whether at work or in our private lives—the people with whom we often associate.

You may be thinking, "That's easy for you to say, Jeanne, but you should meet some of the people I work with in my company. There is not a person with a sense of humor in the bunch." Or as one man told me after a speech, "You should know my boss. I've never seen him crack a smile." Another recounted, "Not a person in our family really likes Aunt So-and-So, but she is certainly always present at the family gatherings." Believe me, I know what you mean. You should see some of the people I encounter traveling from speech to speech. And, of course, every family has a so-and-so. That is why the magic trick is to be aware of the humor levels of people around you, and when given the choice, spend time with those who have a sense of humor. Let them influence you. If associating with those individuals is not always convenient or possible, make up your mind that others will not affect your thinking in a negative manner.

I have a number of business and personal friends I can count on to boost my spirits and bring a smile to my face. They might not even realize they influence me to keep a sense of humor, but I am very aware of the pleasure of being around them, and I make it a point to spend time with them. They play major roles in my desire to continue to develop my own sense of humor.

We usually do not have to look far to find these types of humorous thinkers. There are plenty of them around. They could be in the next office or on the same committee. They might be active in our churches or the parents of our child's best friend. Perhaps they are even . . . right next door.

Until several years ago, I lived next door to a person who personified the meaning of humor as a lifestyle. Her name is Janice Pulliam, and I regretted it when she moved away. It was always a pleasure to be around her because she had such a knack of laughing at herself and the everyday situations in her life. She also delighted in creating harmless humor from time to time. Of course, when you have a life like Janice's, I guess one develops a sense of humor in order to survive.

Whenever I told people in Burlington I lived next to Janice Pulliam, they smiled. Some burst out laughing. Actually, she is rarely called by her full name. "Crazy Janice" is usually sufficient.

The facts tell the story.

Oblique Feat

People in the area still talk about the time Janice got her car turned completely sideways in her garage. Common sense tells us that if a person gets a car turned sideways, she can surely get it turned back straight. Wrong. Professional garage people had to come with all their equipment, and eventually, the garage door had to be removed to get the car out.

Yuletide Aftermath

There was the night in late December when Janice single-handedly pulled more than twenty Christmas trees from all over the neighborhood and piled them up in the driveway of the neighbor on the other side of her house.

Political Heat

This same next-door neighbor referred to above was very opposed to a certain political candidate. Two days before the election, Janice obtained a campaign poster of that candidate, put a ladder to the neighbor's house, and secured the poster high on his roof. Then, one by one, she borrowed all the ladders in the neighborhood and took them to a friend's house several blocks away. A sign found on top of your house for a politician you do not like is bad enough, but not being able to find a single ladder in the neighborhood in order to get the sign down, only added fuel to the fire.

Dead End

Some things Janice planned meticulously, but more often, unusual things seemed to just happen to her, and she always rolled with the punches. That's why people like to be around her so much.

For example, take the time she was driving from nearby Greensboro back to Burlington on an old two-lane road. Five of our local women friends were in the car with her. They had been shopping most of the day and packages were stashed in every spare inch of the automobile. They were just riding along, talking, and had just about gotten back to Burlington when someone commented that the traffic certainly was heavy.

"It's unbelievable," Janice agreed. "The people in front of me are going so slow I can't get around them, and some man behind me has been sitting on my bumper since Greensboro. He wants to pass me so badly that he's got his lights on!"

The passengers turned to look.

"My, God, Janice!" someone screamed from the back seat. "We're in a funeral procession!"

Five women started giving instructions.

"Cut on your lights."

"Pull over."

"Turn off at the next road!"

Janice said, "The next road is the cemetery! The policeman is motioning us in."

"Tell him we're not with this group."

"Do you want to tell him?"

Silence.

So while five women did their best to control their shock, laughter, and disbelief, Janice nodded politely to the officer, and pulled into the cemetery with the procession. The comments started again. "I can't believe this."

"I don't have on a hat."

"Pull to the left and we'll visit another grave."

But when the car came to a stop in the line of traffic, they ceased talking.

People began getting out of the other cars while our group sat in a state of semi-shock. Finally someone said, "Now what?"

Janice said, "We can't just sit here. Get out. Just stand by the car . . . and bow your heads."

It is amazing how people follow instructions in a time of crisis. I know these women. They are intelligent, rational people; but all five of them got out with Janice and stood silently by her car during the grave-side service. Needless to say, they were the first ones back in their automobile when it was over—their bodies hurting from restraining laughter. By that point, of course, the seriousness of the situation had also taken over. They sat quietly and waited for their turn to leave. It was as though they knew that if anyone said a word, they would all "lose it."

Janice was the first one to finally speak. With tears rolling down her face as she pulled her car out of the cemetery, she said, "He . . . or she . . . was such a good person."

. . . they don't let Janice drive on the "big roads" anymore.

Farcical Flap

Not long after the funeral procession episode, Janice had another opportunity to keep her sense of humor. She took her son to play tennis early one evening, and then turned back by her house to tell her husband J.C. something before running several errands. Leaving the car in the driveway, she had to go all the way upstairs to find him. He was in the shower and could not hear her shouts. She finally got the message to him, and about five minutes after arriving, left the house to find her car . . . gone!

Janice later swore she did not leave the car running, but admitted she left the key in the car. "I was only going to be gone a FEW minutes," she explained.

J.C. was still in the shower, so Janice swung into action. Screaming to him over the running water what had happened, she raced to the telephone and called the local police. She identified herself, gave her address, and shouted into the phone, "Our silver Mercedes has been stolen within the last ten minutes! If you can get a bulletin out right now, you can probably catch the thief before he gets out of town!" She was not thinking rationally. Within ten minutes, the thief could be long gone out of our town.

Someone began ringing the doorbell while Janice was giving the license number to Police Headquarters. By that point J.C.— dripping wet—had on his underwear and opened the door while at the same time standing behind it, crouching over and peeping around to see who was there.

Richard Lawson from across the street was standing on the porch. "We can't get out of our front door," he said. "Your car is in the way!"

"Janice!" J.C. shouted. Janice was hanging up the phone. "JAN-ICE! THE CAR IS IN RICHARD LAWSON'S FRONT YARD!"

Janice raced to a front window and looked out across the street. There in the neighbor's front yard was the silver Mercedes, backed onto their front steps.

The three of them stood there a few seconds while the shock of what happened sunk in. The car had just rolled out of the driveway, across the street, over the curb, and into the Lawson's yard. It would have still been rolling if the porch steps had not been in the way.

Then it hit them. "My gosh," J.C. said, "the police! Call the police and tell them to cancel the order!" Janice tripped over furniture getting to the telephone, but it was too late. Let it never be said that Burlington's finest is not on the ball. A squad car pulled into the driveway as she put her hand on the receiver.

By now Richard was in the house, and the three of them watched out the foyer window as policemen in three squad cars slammed on brakes in front of the house. One officer practically bounded out of his car and raced to the front door. The others began to look around the driveway for clues.

Still standing behind the front door and by now stepping into his jeans, J.C. said, "O.K. Dingbat. You got us into this mess . . ." Richard said nothing. He was estimating damage to his yard and porch steps.

When Janice opened the door, she was confronted by a very young, nice-looking, eager officer. He had his tablet and pen out and was ready for the facts. Later she said that she thought it was his first case.

"Are you the lady who called about the stolen silver Mercedes?" he began.

Janice fought to hold back her laughter. It did not help that she could hear her husband and neighbor snickering behind the door.

"Yes sir," she answered. Her mind was racing.

"How long has the car been gone?"

"About fifteen minutes," she said. He wrote it down. "Can you give me a description of the vehicle?"

"I can do better than that, officer," Janice said in her most pitiful, humble voice. "If you turn around and look over there, you can get the description yourself."

The young officer turned and saw the Mercedes resting on the front porch steps in the yard across the street.

Janice was tugging at his sleeve. "Do you HAVE to report this?"

By now he was laughing. "Yes, ma'am. We've already put out a bulletin on it."

"Will it be in the newspaper?" she asked.

"If not," he answered with a grin, as he put his tablet in his pocket, "I'll make sure to tell everyone I see." And then he added, "Lady, you've made my day."

Dial-A-Laugh

. . . and then there was the night Janice and J.C. left one of their cars on the street in front of their house. Around two A.M., a teenager sped down the street and crashed into their parked car, knocking it up in the yard into a tree. Fortunately, the boy was not hurt. The crash woke everyone in the neighborhood except Janice and J.C., who slept through all the commotion.

As the crowd gathered around the automobile, it became apparent the car was a total loss, and it did not look good for the tree. The general discussion eventually centered around that, and how the news should be broken to the owners. How do you let a couple know something like this at two in the morning? Do you just ring their doorbell, or throw rocks at their windows, or what? Since we live in North Carolina, someone suggested we pull a Gomer Pyle, stand under their bedroom window and all sing out, "Sur'prise! Sur'prise! Sur'prise!"

Finally, the neighbor on the other side of Janice's house, of Christmas tree and political poster fame, said he would go inside and just call them. While everyone waited by the wrecked car, he went home to telephone. He dialed the number and waited. After several rings someone finally picked up the receiver, but did not say a word. Instead, what he heard was VERY HEAVY, LABORED breathing. He was so startled he sat there a few seconds and listened as the breathing got louder and more intense. Finally he spoke very slowly, "Jan-ice?"

Janice quickly responded, "Oh, it's you. I glanced at my clock and figured anyone calling this time of night had to be an OBSCENE CALLER. I wanted to GET THE JUMP ON HIM!"

It is a never ending story. You too may have neighbors or friends that remind you of Janice. When given a chance, associate with neighbors and friends who have good senses of humor.

Power of Association

After sixteen years of handling the business end of my speaking career, my husband Jerry and I decided it was time to hire someone to help me in my office. I needed a person who could type and answer the telephone, someone with skills to deal with the public. Also, I needed someone who had a good sense of humor.

I had noticed a woman, Toni Meredith, who was very active in volunteer work in our town, and wondered if she might be interested in making a little money. (The choice of the word "little" was not accidental.) Toni told me on the telephone that she had the clerical skills needed for the position, and I knew from talking to people and to Toni that she could certainly meet the public. But how does one judge a sense of humor during an interview? A couple of days later, she came over.

To get a flavor of the interview, one must understand about my office at that point in my career. At that time I was running my speaking business out of a very small, spare bedroom in my home. It also doubled as a laundry area. The day Toni came for an interview, stacks of clean and dirty laundry were all over the room. The stacks were always present and were constantly getting mixed. Sometimes I washed clothes three or four times before they made it out of the room. I saw no need in presenting an abnormal working environment to a potential associate. So I left everything as it was, and told her to pull up a stack of towels and have a seat.

As our interview discussion progressed, I stressed to Toni that even though we ran JSR, Inc. from a spare room in my home, we needed to have a businesslike, official-sounding, office approach, as much as possible. There was no need for a client in some faraway city to know the phone was occasionally under a stack of dirty jeans, or that if either of us moved in the office we bumped into the other. "Oh, I can do that," Toni assured me. Somehow, I sensed she could. As we talked further, the telephone rang and I reached for it. "Wait," she said. "Let me get it."

Toni picked up the telephone and immediately turned into executive secretary of the year. In a very businesslike voice she said, "Good Morning. Jeanne Robertson's office. This is Toni Meredith. May I help you?" She had turned into such an efficient person so quickly that I started getting tickled, especially when I heard her say, "I'm not sure if Mrs. Robertson is in yet this morning. I've just arrived. The light indicating her arrival is not turned on, but sometimes she comes into her office through the back outside entrance. If you'll hold, I'll walk back there and check." She put the receiver down, and I doubled up with laughter and fell over on the sofa as I buried my face in a pillow.

Toni then proceeded to walk to the closet . . . carefully stepping over a cardboard box of files . . . and opened the door before I could warn her. An odd assortment of things tumbled down on her head, but she quickly pushed them back up, looked around the closet, shut the door, and returned to the phone. I bit into a towel to keep from laughing out loud.

When she again picked up the receiver, she became serious immediately and said, "Well, we're in luck. Mrs. Robertson IS in. If you'll hold a second, I'll transfer the call." With that, she shoved the receiver toward me. By now tears were rolling down my face from laughter, but I was not to be outdone. I pulled myself together as best I could and managed to say, "This is Jeanne Robertson. How may I help you?"

And a male voice said, "This is Jerry Robertson. Is somebody over there going to be able to take my shirts to the cleaners?"

Touché

There should be little doubt I hired Toni Meredith that day, and over ten years later she's still plugging away—although she has become a little picky about sitting on the stacks of laundry. By making the decision that humor was an important quality in the person running my office—a person I would be associating with on a daily basis—I have been able to further develop my own sense of humor. Of course, I loved it when Toni had been working for me less than two weeks, and a local woman whom we both knew called. Toni dutifully took the message and was just getting ready to identify herself to the caller when the lady closed the conversation. When I later returned the call, the woman said, "By the way, your maid sounded halfway intelligent."

Candid Banter

On one occasion, I was running late getting ready to fly to California for a speaking engagement. It was one of those days when everything happened at once, and I was struggling to keep my sense of humor. O.K. Quite frankly, my sense of humor had been momentarily misplaced. Toni came in and I practically started screaming, "I don't think I'll make it this time! I must be on that plane to California in less than two hours! I'm not packed! I'm not going to be able to return these phone calls." Suddenly I stopped in my tracks. Toni was just staring up at me. (She's only five feet tall.) I solicited a promise. "Toni, if I go stark-raving mad, rip off all my clothes, and run through the streets of Burlington, North Carolina, promise me you won't let the women around here talk about me after the doctors come in their white jackets and take me away." Toni casually sat down at the desk and leaned back in the chair, as though in deep thought, before she finally spoke. "Why don't you just wait until you get to California to do that? Nobody out there will even notice you."

Friendly Ruse

Toni and I were having trouble with a particular piece of mechanical office equipment. We attempted to repair it with an odd assortment of tools ranging from nail files to steak knives, but it became apparent our efforts were futile. With warranty in hand, we drove to Greensboro to the nearest repair center. Toni took the machine inside while I circled the block. I circled and circled. Finally, she reappeared carrying the machine with her.

"I had a little trouble. They didn't want to honor the warranty," she explained as she eased into the front seat of the car.

"Why not? It hasn't expired."

"Red tape," she answered matter-of-factly. "Massive red tape. And I don't think I handled the situation very well. The man in charge acted very ugly to me."

"Ugly? Was it a bad scene?"

"It wasn't pleasant. I kept trying to explain the problem to him but he kept snapping at me. Finally, I told him I would never be back in his shop, and he could take the rest of his machines and go jump in a lake."

"Toni! You didn't! You've got to deal with that guy. You don't want him upset with you."

"Oh, relax. He doesn't know who I am," she answered. And after an appropriate pause, she mumbled . . . "I told him I was you."

Needless to say, the machine in her hands was a loaner. The merchant had graciously taken ours in for repair.

See what I mean about associating with people with a sense of humor?

As One Thinketh!

When Toni announced that she would be spending her Friday night at a Quiet Riot rock concert in Greensboro with seven fourteen-year-old girls, I realized it was a situation I could not let pass. "Take notes," I pleaded. "Think of yourself as a humorist and write down everything you think is funny. Get ideas for me." She agreed. The next day she called with her report.

"1. Carol Davis and I were the only older people except employees at the coliseum.

2. One older man working there talked to us. Others didn't even see us, except for a teenage usher who offered Carol cotton for her ears.

3. A souvenir man offered to save two buttons for me, and I went back and purchased them to put into Andy and Lesley's stockings at Christmas.

4. Quiet Riot was scheduled to appear at 10:15 P.M. and finally came on at 11:30 P.M., by which time everyone seem to be well-worked into a wild frenzy.

5. The buttons fell out of my purse on the way home, and I went ahead and gave them to the kids. That's about it."

"That's all? Let me get this straight. You were there over five hours, and that's . . . about it?"

"No, one more thing. I THINK the lead singer was a girl."

Imagineering in Process

At one point in time, the National Speakers Association had an elaborate Mentor/Mentee Program in which more experienced speakers assisted newer platform personalities. The year before the program was initiated, I met a speaker, Gail Wenos, from California who used ventriloquism to illustrate her points. She asked me several questions about advancing her professional speaking career, we corresponded for several months, and later worked together in the Mentor/Mentee program.

I came in the office one day to find that she had sent an audio cassette of one of her ventriloquist programs, and had written asking that I listen and send any helpful suggestions. Toni was already grinning from ear to ear. "An AUDIO cassette of a ventriloquist?" she exclaimed. "You're gonna critique an AUDIO cassette of a ventriloquist? How will you know if she's any good? It will be like critiquing an audio cassette of a tap dancer."

We started playing the cassette to find that not only could we understand the program, but that the woman was good—very good. But Toni couldn't resist one more jab.

About fifteen minutes into the cassette she stood up and said, "I've got to get back to work. The woman's good, but if you want my opinion . . . she moves her lips too much!"

Toni is a prime example of a person who places a high priority on a humorous attitude. Over the course of time and because of a desire to associate with people like Toni, I have also developed a number of friends in my profession who share my philosophy concerning humor as a lifestyle. Many of my best friends are also humorists, although certainly not all. More importantly, their senses of humor do not cease when they turn off the microphones. It is these folks I try to associate with because they help my sense of humor stay intact and grow.

Don't Look Now

One of my speaker buddies who places a priority on humor is Linda Pulliam. Linda lives in Chapel Hill, North Carolina, and I know I can always count on her to brighten my day with something humorous. When we were to meet on a flight in Dallas to continue to a convention in San Francisco, I boarded the plane to find her dressed for success, casually sitting in the first class section reading a magazine . . . and wearing one of those sets of fake eye glasses with a huge plastic nose and black mustache attached. Naturally, I did not say a word . . . just put up my things and sat down. For about five minutes we sat there quietly, nonchalantly faking interest in non-interesting magazines while dozens of passengers walked by our seats. Without looking up, she finally leaned toward me and spoke, causing the big fake mustache to lift with each word. "I can understand you not reacting, but don't you think it's fascinating that not a single one of the other passengers has said a word?"

Kookie Cook

Of all the people I know who don't cook, including myself, Linda falls into a category all by herself. Every once in a while she gives it a try and usually shares her results with friends. Fortunately, she has such a good sense of humor, I can write about those occasions. One night when we were invited to dinner, we pulled into their driveway to see smoke billowing from every window. We knew that meant Linda was cooking another meal. We were thrilled because we knew the food would at least be hot. The time before, she served stone-cold Mexican food which she purchased at a restaurant that afternoon. She could have heated it, but the microwave wasn't working and, as she put it, "the stove takes too long to warm up."

The week before Christmas she brought over a pumpkin pie. I was most impressed but cautious. Beaver bit into a piece and then put down his fork and asked, "Why does she keep trying?" The pie sat in the refrigerator until January 17th, which gave it a shelf life of about a month. I was leaving town that morning on a speaking trip and suddenly remembered it was a friend's birthday. I did not have time to buy a cake or pie, so I just wrote a little note. "Happy Birthday. Was going to make you a pie but didn't have time. Hope you enjoy this one we've had since before Christmas. We didn't like it, but you never know . . . ."

I left the pie and note in Norma White's kitchen, drove to Greensboro and caught a flight to Milwaukee. Since Norma is one of my best friends—as well as a closet humorist living incognito in Burlington as a high school math teacher—I thought she would appreciate my efforts. But at this point, I started worrying about food poisoning. When I changed planes in Chicago, I frantically called back and left a message for Norma not to eat the pie. "It could be dangerous. I'll explain when I return."

Later Norma said my call had been unnecessary. She and husband Alan knew better than to eat the pie. Not only did the pie look absolutely horrible (she claimed she put it in the refrigerator and food beside it tried to jump to other shelves), but Norma saw Linda's name on the bottom of the dish. A small detail. Later Linda claimed she bought the pie at a bazaar and put it in her pie pan, but her explanation fell on deaf ears. That's what happens when you are a legend in your own time.

Of course, I mentioned to Norma that I could have made the pie and just put it in a pie pan of Linda's that was at my house. She said she had thought of that, but it didn't matter. She wasn't eating a pie cooked by either one of us!

Holiday Deliverance

It was that same holiday that the normally humorous, upbeat Linda faced a real challenge. Her only child, daughter Kim, was away from home for the first time over Christmas. I did what I could. Took over two boxes of old, dirty tree ornaments and some tacky plastic decorations. New decorations do not bring smiles. A box of pitiful ones will do the trick. All this helped for a while, but Linda and husband Charles decided to tackle the problem head-on and go away on a Christmas trip. Shortly before the new year, just when we were all fighting the general physical and mental collapse from the holiday rush, Linda's other friends and I received the following letter, printed verbatim, of her account of their 1988 Christmas Holidays:

> The Christmas of '88 will L-O-N-G be remembered. This being the first Christmas we've spent in a "non-traditional" fashion.
>
> Kim is in Germany. Timely to start a new tradition. A tradition where Charles and I celebrate the holidays in some adventuresome fashion. First mistake.
>
> We made elaborate plans to go skiing in West Virginia. Never having been skiing, we didn't know what to expect. We DID expect snow. As we rolled up to the "rustic lodge" (clever way to describe genuine laminated pine wood paneling and prefab fireplace) it was 54 degrees and raining. Not one bit of snow. Seems they had neglected to change the recorded ski condition report. Second mistake.

Being the flexible souls we are, we decided to have a good time anyway. We walked through the mud and looking up at the slopes we could almost imagine people having a grand old time whizzing past. Almost. We worked up quite an appetite on the walk back to the lodge. Somehow the bus forgot to come back for us and the 4 mile walk back to the lodge really gave our appetites an edge. A trend was developing.

The dining room was splendid with brilliant plastic poinsettias and shimmering tinsel tree. Without my glasses, it almost looked festive. Guess most people spend Christmas the way we always had done, with friends and family. There was only one other couple at the lodge. We were looking forward to meeting them at dinner. Unfortunately, they had some sort of misunderstanding right before their meal was served and the woman left immediately after she threw her dinner roll at the man.

After getting "sorry, there's not any _____ tonight . . . nope we're out of that too . . ." (the kitchen staff was a skeleton crew and may have even been the waitress herself!)—we asked "What DO you have?" Delicious corn chowder. O.K., anybody can have turkey and dressing with all the trimmings. After all, this was destined to be a "different" holiday, right? Biggest mistake.

Approximately one hour after the corn chowder, it occurred to us that we might need to know how to get to the nearest hospital. Since I was the one who chose the chef's choice, I was the one with food poisoning. All Christmas Eve and on into the wee hours of the morning, I was putting my life in order, in case '89 never arrived. We spent that most wonderful night of the year in an 8 × 10 "rustic" room with an unforgettable red shag rug. The red rug is an entirely different story. From time to time Charles would softly whistle a little carol. He's a good man. When physically possible, I'd nibble another corner from the 4 saltine crackers the waitress so generously sold us.

A good friend, Jeanne Robertson, knew the potential difficulties of this holiday away from home. Having an only child, she could imagine what we might have in store. With the sensitivity and special understanding only a few possess, she gave me a gift to be opened at the ski "resort." At one of the lowest moments of the evening, Charles perked up and said, "Hey, you haven't opened Jeanne's gift yet! Bet that'll cheer you up." I rallied for a moment. With my loving mate's assistance, propped up on pillows and wadded ski jackets, we opened the gift. It was a small, black plastic spider. The evening was unsalvageable.

Mid morning Christmas day, we limped to the dining room. The other couple had checked out. Disappointing. After a big bowl of fresh corn flakes (so much for the chef)—we checked out. Things were looking up.

Life rarely turns out exactly as we plan. To enjoy it ONLY when everything's according to schedule and on target makes as much sense as to write off a Christmas that didn't have snow or turkey.

It was a wonderful Christmas. We have our health, each other, a few good friends and the sense to be grateful for it all.

—Linda

Special note: It was a VERY NICE black plastic spider. My friend Norma, who had the good sense not to eat the pumpkin pie, liked her spider.

Asphalt Jungle

The routine pressures associated with the job were mounting on me as my year as President of the National Speakers Association drew to a close. I thought I had handled the responsibilities of the position fairly well and kept my sense of humor through most of it, but I had one week to go and was caught up in the busy national convention. The pace had taken its toll. I was tired.

The members of the National Speakers Association are very vocal, not only from the platform, but also to their board of directors. During our very hectic convention—held in Scottsdale, Arizona, at a lovely resort—I was practically accosted in the hotel lobby by a woman who had a complaint. She grabbed me by the arm while she explained she was allergic to the asphalt around the hotel. She was most adamant in her belief that the board of directors should have checked out something like that. She even insinuated a law suit. I was taken aback and forgot to use humor. I twisted my arm loose and mumbled something like, "I'll bring it up at the next board meeting and I hope you feel better," and moved on through the lobby.

A couple of minutes later, I ran into Al Walker from Columbia, South Carolina, a buddy whom I always like to be around. He certainly has a humorous attitude. I was a little flustered—O.K., practically foaming at the mouth—and said, "Some nut just told me the board of directors should have known she was allergic to the asphalt around the hotel!"

Without a second's hesitation, Al quipped, "You should have said, 'We knew it! We just wanted to see you bloat up!'"

Ah . . . the beauty of associating with people who see life through humorous eyes.

Cordial Companions

Of the thousands of speakers I know, among my closest friends are three other humorists: Doc Blakely, Robert Henry, and Joe Griffith. In 1979, we began working together in a group we call the Platform Professionals. Newt Hielscher, whose idea it was to form the group initially, was also an associate until his retirement. It is by choice that we send written monthly reports to each other (usually humorous), assist each other with creating new material, and in general work to further each of our careers while still maintaining separate offices and businesses in different areas of the country. In 1987, we coauthored *How The Platform Professionals KEEP 'EM LAUGHIN'* (published by Rich Publishing Co.), a book on how to put humor in speeches. Doc says it is in its third printing because the first two were blurry. (Actually, the second printing came off the presses in March 1989, and the third is expected to follow as soon as we read all of those.)

The Platform Professionals choose to be associates because of a common humor philosophy. This support system of people, along with their spouses and staff members, view the world through humorous eyes, and it is to these people I often turn when my sense of humor needs a pickup. They think like I think. At times, that can be a scary thought . . . for all involved. We do not have a formal working agreement as often exists with a group of business associates, but the association with cohorts in the humor business allows us to share a common interest and to work magic on our senses of humor.

Speaker's Nightmare

You read about Robert Henry in the last section. He is the speaker whom we convinced had to give his keynote address slot to President Reagan. I thought you might enjoy an excerpt from one of his monthly reports to Doc, Joe, and me. It speaks for itself.

> To: Platform Professionals
> From: Robert Henry
> Subject: Recent tragic speaking experience.
>
> The job on February 15th was a nightmare.
>
> I went in the room an hour early to set up my wireless mike. That sucker worked perfectly. I went to the reception. I went back to the banquet room and checked it again. Perfect! Fifteen minutes before we were to start, I checked it a third time. It worked so well I decided I didn't need a backup system.
>
> A beauty queen stepped forward to introduce me. She was using the band's sound system which had speakers the size of Volkswagons. When I flipped on my transmitter, the speakers began to squall and three pacemakers went out.
>
> The wireless system wouldn't work so I rushed forward to the beauty queen and grabbed her mike which belonged to the band. I did my opening poem—a guaranteed show stopper and they responded as if I had led them in the Lord's Prayer and three Hail Marys.

Two minutes into the speech and I'm fighting for my life. Three drunks began to yell, "We can't hear." I'm standing in the middle of a decibel field that has removed most of the hair from my body and these drunks can't hear.

I had to stop everything, go behind stage, get on hands and knees and attempt to readjust a sound system that had worked beautifully an hour earlier. I figured this would be a great time for a necrology report, but the guy who kept the records was one of those who had passed and there was no trustworthy list as to who was alive and who wasn't. My observation was that half of the audience was ready for entombment.

I got the wireless mike working. The problem was the band's system which was sending out RF's that probably nullified NATO's radar net.

I ran back to the dance floor to be met by a room of silence in which a Tibetan Monk would be proud to live.

I once heard a speaker say he loved the really rough ones—the hard nuts to crack—the hostile audiences it takes 20 minutes to begin to move. It's this type of idiotic reasoning that has kept that fellow the greatest secret on the American platform.

Suddenly, a drunk stood up and began to yell at me. He was a world class yeller. I went to him to try to show him I was on his side. He put his head on my chest to yell into my mike and drooled Jack Daniels on a $35 silk tie.

I used Newt Hielscher's jackass story and it worked, the audience roared with approval. I thought I had won them over. Not so! They began to slip perilously close to a coma.

I went for the big one, the best bit I've got. Guaranteed to convulse everyone within earshot.

In the middle of the joke, my mind went blank—I mean nothing. I couldn't remember what joke I was setting up. I mumbled something incoherent about getting my fingers around the throat of any speaker who professed to like the "really rough ones."

After all of that, half a dozen confused folks came forward to tell me it was a wonderful speech. Oh well, next time a speaker says he "likes the hostile audiences is takes 20 minutes to begin to move," I'll tell him about a tough group in Savannah he'll love.

Quick-Witted

Doc Blakely from Wharton, Texas, is another member of our group and is known for his quick wit. One Sunday afternoon I received a call from Doc, and before we hung up, he said, "Well, are you busy this week?" Speakers like to know if other speakers are busy.

"Yes," I answered, "I spoke to the VIPs of Alamance County earlier this afternoon, and I go out in the morning." Notice the way I brushed over "VIPs." I knew it had whetted his interest and I could practically see him mulling over what I said. "You gonna be busy, Doc?"

"Yes, I'll be out of town." He paused. "The VIPs?" he said. "You spoke on Sunday afternoon? That's a little unusual. What was that group?"

"The V-I-Ps," I responded slowly. "Tell Pat hello for me."

"Sure, I'll tell her. I don't believe I've ever heard of the VIPs. Who are they?"

Enough was enough. "The VIPs are the Visually Impaired Persons of my county," I admitted.

"Aha!" he said without a moment's hesitation. "There's a group you'll be able to convince you were in the Miss America Pageant!"

Compassion or Cash

The last of our little group known as Platform Professionals is Joe Griffith from Dallas, Texas. Joe is a real character and has been a full-time professional speaker for years. You would remember him if you had heard one of his funny presentations, but that might not be the case if you've seen him on one of his many TV commercials. He's got one of those run-of-the-mill, middle-America, nondescript, "you won't remember it" faces that is perfect for selling things like . . . tires. Joe is particularly good at creating humor, and of the many examples I could relate, my favorite is an experience Joe had in the Navy in the sixties. It illustrates the way Joe thinks, and is a good example of his great sense of humor that has continued to grow through the years.

In 1964, Joe found himself approaching Christmas aboard the USS Yorktown, an aircraft carrier patrolling the Pacific area. Always the type to start things rolling, he talked two buddies into sending the following letter to eighteen newspapers in the States:

> We are three sailors aboard a carrier in the Western Pacific. We receive very little mail and one of us has no family to write. During the holiday season, would you please print our names in your newspaper so that someone might take a few minutes to write one, or maybe all, of us?

Naturally, many newspapers printed the appeal, and before the scenario ended, the boys received over 25,000 letters, 3500 in one day. Joe recalls that particular day when three sacks of mail were delivered to the ship, and all of the letters were for them. When he told me about the story, I asked to see the press clippings. As we looked at the many articles, he started laughing, and said, "Every one of those letters was answered."

"You're kidding. You must have been very, very lonely."

"Not really," he said, grinning from ear to ear. "We sold the letters to other guys on board."

Friendly Chiding

Still yet another speaker friend is Ed Kelsay (yes, the one in on the Robert Henry/President Reagan episode). Ed is the Legal Counsel for the Oklahoma State Medical Association and is also a humorist. He sent the following cover letter to Doc, Joe, and me, along with a copy of the second letter which went to Robert.

Dear Jeanne, Doc, and Joe,

Your colleague and partner in crime . . . Robert H. Henry . . . gave what was truly a "peak performance" to the Annual Meeting of the Oklahoma State Medical Association May 6.

I have sent him the enclosed letter to promote his services to other medical associations. (About a week from now I'll send him the real one!)

Yours truly,

Ed Kelsay
Legal Counsel

Dear Mr. Henry:

Thank you for the nice little talk that you gave to our organization recently. I had one or two people come up to me and say how much they enjoyed it, even though they did have difficulty understanding you because of your accent.

I am sure that you would like to know that the president-elect's wife will not have a permanent scar from the pot of hot coffee that you knocked into her lap. However, the hotel did charge us $385 for the curtain that caught fire when you knocked over the candelabra.

There's a possibility you may be invited back this winter. I overheard the president and president-elect saying something to the effect that it would "be a cold day . . . ."

There is also a possibility that our president may sue you for slander just because you referred to his wife as, "that bimbo in black," and the young doctor whose wife appeared in the "atomic dress . . . it was mostly fallout," has offered to do some rather unusual surgery on your anatomy. But beyond that, your presentation was adequate.

Please feel free to use this letter whenever you advertise to other medical societies. However, I would prefer that you leave my name off of it.

Yours truly,

Ed

Crony Capers

Linda, Al, and Ed along with the Platform Professionals—Robert, Doc, and Joe—are but a few of my friends in the speaking profession who have created a lifestyle in which humor is a conscious and significant element. Quite frankly, however, they have nothing on my hometown friends, as aptly illustrated by an event I hosted in Alamance County, North Carolina.

I sent the invitation below to sixty-seven women in my home town area and in several other cities in North Carolina. Many of them did not know each other before the party, but I believed that a humorous invitation would set the stage and serve to bring out the humorous side of most of the people. I was correct. How would you have responded if you had received the following invitation?

O.K. GET READY!

YOU'RE INVITED TO AN "INTERESTING CRONY" PARTY!

A good friend of mine, Patricia Fripp, is coming to town and that is a good excuse to have an "event." I hope you will be able to come!

The dinner party will be held on Monday night, January 23rd at the Two For Tea Restaurant in Burlington. We'll begin with a little "gathering" around 7:00 P.M., eat around 7:45 and then take it from there . . . You should be on the way home by 10-10:30ish. If the party gets dull, feel free to leave before then.

Let me share a little history with you to "set the stage." Patricia is a speaker buddy of mine who lives in San Francisco. She's originally from England, an outstanding speaker and of most importance for this occasion . . . a real character. Every time I speak in San Francisco and she is in town, she gathers some of her "interesting cronies" (remember, she's British) and we go to comedy clubs, eat out and discuss our "careers." In the mornings, I walk and she jogs (she's very short & takes little steps compared to mine) while we try to do something about our "rears." Her friends are great, and verrr-ry interesting. Several border on strange. But I've always told her, "Hey, we've got interesting people in North Carolina, too. Not to mention strange."

Well, Patricia's coming to North Carolina for a speech and will whip through here for a couple of days. Her first comments to me when she booked the speech were "I'm coming to Burlington. Get together some of your interesting cronies!" Her second comment was, "Will there be enough people for me to say a few words?" By this point, I know what you are wondering, so let me assure you . . . YOU are asked because you are interesting, not because you are strange. (Pay no attention to the fact this letter of invitation is printed.)

Because we are all so interesting and many will not know each other, we're going to do something a bit unusual to make sure we all have a fun time. I'm sure we've all attended events and sat with people with whom we thought we had little in common, only to discover as we were leaving, that we had a common ground. When you RSVP to Toni, please tell her three of the MANY INTERESTING THINGS about you. If you are shy about this, do not worry, Toni and I will make up something. (Notice the way I just switched the potential blame to Toni. I've had a teenager. I know about shifting the blame.)

I do hope you will be able to come, meet a buddy of mine, and maybe more importantly, get to better know some "cronies" right here in our area.

And if you come, whatever you do . . . be interesting!

Jeanne

Sixty-six women were able to attend. Most of them telephoned or mailed in their three "interesting things," and almost without fail their interesting facts were humorous in nature. I never doubted that would be the case.

The second letter that went to the guests for this party was eight pages long and contained information on dress, the names and addresses of those coming, and . . . their "interesting facts." Many of the responses were humorous if you knew the person or lived in our community. The following are some of the other interesting responses that you may appreciate:

- Lived in Germany for several years after college & the secret "access" word for my savings account at the local bank was "sauerkraut," the only German word I knew when I arrived over there. Unfortunately, the tellers thought that was so funny that they told everyone in town. So much for my secret word.

- Am writing and publishing a best-selling book in the early 1990's. (Maybe this public disclosure will help me get started. Pressure, you know . . . .)

- Am a neophyte organic gardener. Last year when our first "crop" came in, we sat down to enjoy the fruits of our labors. However, when we realized that the salads we were eating cost about $400, we couldn't swallow.

- I'm definitely "overbearing." Mother of nine children.

- In sales and merchandising. Love to put outfits together. Spent an entire day going through Jeanne's closet. Best advice: "Burn everything. Don't even give this stuff away."

- Love antiques and have a furniture consignment shop. Can sell anything. Bring your antiques to me. (No husbands accepted.)

- Can touch the end of my nose with my tongue.

- At a penny a vote, was runner-up to Halloween Queen in the 7th grade. Would have been queen but Daddy wouldn't give five more dollars.

- Make great decorative bows. Drop by anytime with your ribbons. Call ahead during the rushed holiday season.

- Was a registered nurse in Detroit and was set to leave in eight days for a job in Fairbanks, Alaska, when I met a tennis coach from N.C. Became engaged four days later and ditched the job in Alaska. We've been married 20 years.

- As the mother of three—ages 16, 19, and 22—I have been through every sort of public humiliation, all of them expensive, and so far I've come out of it better off than I went in.

- Collect antiques. Am disappointed that any antique may be only half my age.

- Mother of three. Once considered getting a job, but when asked about my experience, just hated to write down "gets out stains well."

- Can whistle & hum at the same time.

- Still have a sweater given to me in the 9th grade.

- Once rode Trigger . . . SURE this group recalls him.

- Own a specialty shop featuring monograms. Will monogram your forehead on a slow day.

- Have a "mixed marriage"—he went to N.C. State, I'm a graduate of the University of North Carolina at Chapel Hill.

- Have a "hippo" fetish. Collect them. The animal, not broad hips . . . although that could be a possibility.

- Am anthropomorphic, which means I attribute human characteristics to things not human . . . such as college students.

- In past ten years have worked in advertising, as a maid, and as a barmaid, all of which I found necessary in opening my own advertising company.

- Played on same high school basketball team with Jeanne . . . thirty years ago. One of the few people who know how much Jeanne has exaggerated her basketball point average through the years.

- Read Town & Country and am a walking Emily Post whose speech is nevertheless peppered with expressions like "fat as a mudball," "I'm so mad I could stomp him through a crack," and "He's already beat my ears back about that."

- Travel all over the country in connection with my publishing company but am also a farmer. Many of you feed children. I feed 500 cows every day I am home. (Author's note: Smart. Cows don't become teenagers.)
- Created and speak my own language.
- Can wrap a parked car around a telephone pole.
- Am carrying Elvis Presley's unborn child. You read it here first!!!

The Perfect Wrap

Needless to say, the party was successful. Most of the women dressed in their finery, and I did, too. That meant, of course, that I wore my possum-skin fur. ("Opossum" for you formal folks.) No, not a possum fur coat . . . a possum skin. One pelt. It was given to me by another friend with a sense of humor, Dr. Gene Long.

Several years earlier my husband and I were playing bridge with Gene and his wife Gray. I had just returned from a National Speakers Association convention and mentioned that several of the women were dressed to the hilt in designer clothes and furs. "I wouldn't mind having a fur," I said. Being a good friend, Gray quickly mumbled, "You deserve one. Everyone knows you do."

"But many of those women specialize in programs on image," Jerry attempted to explain. "They NEED clothes like that. You're a humorist."

I had visions of wearing a potato sack as I stood on stage somewhere. People were shouting, "You look great in that potato sack because you're a humorist!" I glanced around the bridge table and said half-jokingly, "I repeat . . . I WOULD NOT MIND owning a fur." Gray slammed her cards down on the table and said louder than before, "YOU CERTAINLY DESERVE ONE!"

"Well, honey," Jerry said, "we'll start collecting possums on the side of the road . . . ." Such a funny man.

The very next week, Gene was on his way home from the hospital late one night after delivering a baby. (He's an obstetrician. We're not making medical history here.) He saw a dead possum lying on the side of the road, stopped, and slung it in the back of his van.

The following night, Gene skinned the animal while my husband watched the process through the fingers over his eyes. They did this in Gray's den. "We put down newspapers," they told her when she returned home and noticed an interesting aroma among her antiques. "We would have gone outside, but the Duke basketball game was on TV." Well, of course, that explained it.

At that point, the process became simple. They tacked the skin on the side of the Long's house for drying, and in a couple of weeks, Gene sent it somewhere for curing. By the time it got back, it was a soft, beautiful possum pelt. And I had my fur!

Or, as my husband put it, "the PERFECT FUR for a humorist."

Of course . . . I only wear it on special occasions, like the crony party.

Each of the women at the crony party was not only interesting, but also had a sense of humor. Making an effort to associate with people like the ones who attended this event—as well as with friends who will skin a possum and have it tacked on their house for several weeks—has helped me to further develop my own sense of humor.

It's Your Turn to Work Magic

Make a list of all the people with whom you come in contact most frequently, and then identify the humor levels of these individuals. When given a choice, make it a point to spend more time with the individuals on your list who have a good sense of humor. You will discover that associating with people who place a high priority on humor will work magic in developing your own sense of humor.

Potion 5
Influence Others to
Develop a Sense of Humor

C an you really influence others to develop a sense of humor? I believe that the answer to that question is a resounding yes. Humor is a very powerful influence. It serves to help people grow; it is contagious and spreads like the winter flu; the influence builds and strengthens family relationships; and, of course, the process of influencing others enhances your own sense of humor.

Although there are numerous opportunities to influence others to develop a sense of humor, I strongly believe that the best place to begin is in the home. This fervid belief more than likely originated from the humorous influence of my parents during my early years. My folks had terrific senses of humor, which were developed even further through years of being determined to influence their daughters to see the funny side of life. As I illustrated briefly in the first chapter, my parents influenced me to see the humorous side of being unusually tall. Although they never expressed it directly, I know that they believed they could teach me to have a good sense of humor as surely as they could teach me to shoot a basketball or set a table. The following childhood experiences further illustrate the role my parents played in this important area.

Trick or Treat?

Several years ago I read a letter written to one of the well-known advice columnists from a mother of a tall girl. She explained that at Halloween her daughter had gone trick or treating with friends. At one house a woman judged the young girl by her height and proceeded to inform the youngster that she was too old for the annual Halloween activity. The tall, young lady was embarrassed in front of her peers and had returned home in tears. The mother's letter to the columnist went on to report how her daughter had been mistreated and how rude the woman at the door had been.

Granted, the woman at the door was insensitive. She probably spoke without thinking. But I believe the mother of the tall daughter could have reacted in a much better way. It was evident she had lost her humor over what happened. She let the situation "get to her" when she could have used it to influence her tall daughter to keep a sense of humor, and in the process, kept her own humor intact.

When I read the Halloween letter, I was reminded of a similar situation that occurred when I was in junior high school. It illustrates how my mother reacted differently, and not only influenced me to keep my sense of humor, but probably hers as well. It is a good reminder for all of us and is another of the magic potions that work when developing a sense of humor.

When my classmates and I were in the seventh grade, our parents got together and decided that we could go trick or treating one last year. But on Halloween night some of my best friends said that they did not want me to go with them. They said that I was "too big" and stated specifically, "People will think we've got a grownup along and we won't get as much candy." Very typical seventh graders.

I was crushed and went home to tell my mother about it. She listened intently and could have done what many mothers would do. She could have said, "Well, you didn't want to go with them anyway. Stay home and we'll pop some popcorn and have a good time." But she didn't. She was determined to influence me to see the humor in my unusual height.

When I finished telling her what had happened, she rose to her full five-foot-five height, looked up at me and said, "You can go trick or treating, Jeanne. You just have to get the right costume."

The costume turned out to be two sheets. Mother tied one around my waist, and jumping as high as she could, she threw the other one over my head. "Now, you just crouch down low," she said, "and hurry and catch up with everybody."

It was wonderful! I bent my knees, which crouched me down to about half my size, and went right along with the crowd. My friends thought it was hilarious. I did too. It was a great evening because my Mother was determined I would see the humor in the situation, and she influenced me to do so.

At each house we went to, I practically pushed my friends out of the way, rang the doorbell, thrust my sack out and said, "trick or treat" . . . and brought the candy in. My sack was filling up with all sorts of goodies and I was having a ball. As a matter of fact, I was having such a great time that I began to forget to bend my knees and crouch down.

Arriving at one house, I ran ahead of the pack and rang the doorbell. A woman came to the door and there I was, standing a full six feet, two inches under those sheets. I stuck my bag out. "Trick or treat."

The woman took a step back and started grinning as she looked at the mass of sheets from head to toe. Turning her head, she shouted, "John! Come out here and see these two children one on top of the other in a ghost costume!"

I don't know if you have ever walked up a sidewalk trying to wobble under sheets as though you were two people, one sitting on top of the other. It is not easy.

My friends were howling, having arrived at the door just in time to hear the woman's remark. As they continued down the street, I turned and ran the other way toward home, glad that the sheets covered the fact that I was fighting back the tears.

When I told Mother the story, she was faced with an interesting choice. After all, she had tried once, hadn't she? I mention this because as you think about this magic potion in developing humor, you may think of someone you will try to influence to keep a sense of humor. Your children? Someone at work? A neighbor? You may quickly find that your initial efforts are not met with enthusiasm. Well, influencing folks does not always work right away; just like changing your humor awareness may not occur overnight. You have to keep trying.

As a parent now, I also realize how mother's emotions were probably churning by that point. No mother enjoys her child feeling ridiculed, however slightly. Surely now she would say, "You don't need those people. You've got cousins in Alabama! Let's go to the movies." But she didn't. As she listened to what the woman had said, her eyes widened with amazement.

Suddenly she jumped up and ran to the kitchen. I heard her rummaging about as she shouted, "We've been missing the boat!" In a few moments she rushed back . . . carrying a second sack. "From now on," she announced, "you go as two people!"

Within ten minutes, I caught up with my friends, clutching two sacks under the sheets and standing proudly at six feet, two inches tall. At each house, I stuck out one sack with my right hand near my head and in a little high voice said, "Trick or treat." And with my left hand, I stuck out the second sack near my waist and boomed in a deep voice, "TRICK OR TREAT!" I had a wonderful Halloween because my Mother was determined to influence me to keep a sense of humor, and I suspect that determination enabled her to also enjoy the evening.

Oh, one more thing. I went trick or treating every Halloween for years.

Size What?

Example is such a powerful teacher! It came through again and again as my folks kept their humor intact by influencing me to develop my sense of humor. For example, shopping for clothes was a monumental challenge which presented them with many occasions to use humor. By the time I was in junior high, finding shoes and clothes could have been disastrous, but Mother turned it into what today's teenagers would refer to as a "trip." It was a classic example of someone influencing another to keep a sense of humor.

I wish you could have seen Mother taking me shopping. Standing proudly by my waist, she would say to the salesclerk, "I want to get some things here . . . for the BABY," and lovingly glance all the way up at me.

Once a clerk asked, "What size shoe does 'the BABY' wear?" Mother drew herself up to every bit of her 5'5" and said, "SHE WEARS A SEVEN AND HALF . . . but an eleven feels reeeeal gooood if you happen to have any." Turning toward me she added with a wink, "And her little legs don't turn as red." We always laughed when the clerks tried to sell me size 10 shoes because the shoes were "open at the toe." "No," Mother would say. "We don't want her toes out on the cold sidewalk."

They're Wearing Them That Way

Although Mother and I spent a lot of our shopping time looking for shoes, clothes were also a major challenge. Tall Girl Shops were few and far between. We scouted them, but if the clothes did happen to fit, they were usually not the styles for a teenage girl. In the fifties and early sixties, most "tall girl clothes" came in blacks, browns, or navy blues. (Today, of course, we also have that exciting color, taupe.) I suspected there was a big tub in New York City where people dyed tall girl clothes and size eleven shoes all at the same time. Of course, there were two good things about that situation. First of all, at least my clothes were coordinated with the colors of my shoes. Secondly, when one of the relatives died, I always had a stylish black or navy dress to wear to the funeral—no matter what season of the year it was. My great-grandmother "lingered" for four years, and Mother had to buy my sisters a new, dark outfit each season. I was always ready.

Other than the black, Tall Girl Shop funeral dresses, Mother made almost all my clothes. Every once in a while, however, we would try the regular clothing stores where we received a variety of advice from well-meaning salesladies. Looking back, I realize how Mother influenced my thinking—and, in turn, hers—in these situations. What could have been awkward shopping afternoons, turned out to be sources of funny stories to be told at that night's dinner. Mother took on the role of the saleslady. I played myself.

"Put your hands on your waist, darlin'," Mother would drawl at dinner, mimicking one of the salesladies who tried to sell us a dress that was just too short-waisted. "I need to see where your waistline is located."

"My waistline is right here, ma'am," I chimed in, placing my hands in the proper place.

"No, no, noooo, darlin', THAT'S not your waistline," Mother continued, grabbing my hands as the lady had done. "Your waistline is here."

"No, no, noooo, ma'am. Those are my . . . ribs."

The rest of the family would be in hysterics, which was all we needed . . . an audience.

"Here, darlin'," Mother continued. "I DO BE'LIEVE if you put this six-inch-wide belt with that dress, it will conceal the fact that the waistline is three inches too high. Don't worry about not being able to breathe. You're going to look SO GOOD . . . right before you pass out."

Mother knew there were just some things we had to purchase in the stores, and she was determined to use humor to help me through what could have been embarrassing excursions. It was as though while we shopped, we lived our own private little comedy sitcoms. Mother was influencing by example, example, example.

One particular shopping trip to a regular store stands out. I tried on a dress that I desperately wanted and was trying my best to scrunch up my body so Mother would think the dress fit. It did not. There I stood . . . in front of a full-length mirror that stopped at my neck, trying on a dress with long sleeves which stopped an inch and a half above my wrists.

"They're wearing the sleeves pushed up this year, dear, so this is JUST RIGHT for you," the saleslady gushed, as she pushed the sleeves toward my elbows. "Just keep your arms bent so the sleeves will not fall back down," she whispered to me.

I wanted the dress so badly, I kept my arms bent and turned to Mother. "That's true. All the sleeves ARE pushed up this year."

"Nooooo, I don't think so," Mother pondered aloud. "I like for long sleeves to be . . . looong sleeves." She straightened one of my arms and the sleeve dropped down.

The saleslady knew I needed some help. "I know what you can do," she said, and rushed to the jewelry counter and back. "Put these bracelets on each arm, honey, and no one will notice the sleeves are a little short." Then, in a reassuring voice she added to Mother, "They are wearing a lot of bracelets this year. It is shown in ALL the fashion magazines." I am sure by that point, Mother wanted to tell the saleslady to throw the bracelets—and the dress—out the window. But she let the scene play its course. Her mind must have been whirling, because there I stood . . . in front of the same full-length mirror that stopped at my neck, both arms bent at the elbows, and wearing a dress with supposedly long sleeves that came right below those elbows and met a row of seven bracelets on each arm. I tried not to look at Mother because by then even I knew I looked ridiculous. The question was, should I laugh or cry?

Finally, Mother caught my eye as she ran her hand along all the bracelets, pretending to admire them. "Jeanne, these just look won-der-ful, but do you know what this outfit needs to be AB-SO-LUTE-LY PERFECT? Open-toed shoes! Then your toes can drag along on the sidewalk and people will not notice the clanking of all these bracelets."

A few minutes later, holding back our laughter, we left the store. A perplexed saleslady was looking through the window at us as she held the dress . . . and fourteen bracelets.

It's a Crying Shame

I thought about Mother and her determination to influence me after a particular speech in Georgia. A woman approached me eager to talk.

"Oh, I wish my daughter could meet you," she began. "She's *so* tall. Five-foot nine in her stocking feet. Of course we try to keep her in low heels."

"Why? If high heels are the style . . . "

"Well, you know. There's no need in adding inches. I measure her every week, but I'm afraid she's still growing."

"Every week? How old is your daughter, ma'am?"

"Well, she's fifteen, but she looks much older because of that height."

"I'm six feet, two inches," I replied, "and I'm sure you realize from my speeches that I consider my height to be an advantage because . . . "

"We don't know where she gets her size. Tell me, are the other people in your family normal?"

"Only during the week."

"I beg your pardon? Oh . . . well, my daughter wears a size 10 shoe and I'm scared to death her feet are still growing. If I've told her once, I've told her a thousand times, she better not grow to a size 11. We won't be able to find a decent pair of shoes."

"I wear a size 11 and finding shoes is not always easy, but . . . "

"It's not just her feet. It's difficult keeping her in decent clothes in dark colors. Bright colors draw attention to a person, and you know what they say about stripes. I always try to keep her in stripes going around to cut her height."

"I can solve the clothes problem for you. There are several good tall girl shops in Charlotte and Atlanta. I'll be happy to send you a list. You could make one trip and . . . "

"Well-l-l, that's a possibility. But it's an awfully long drive, just for clothes."

Pictures flashed through my mind of Mother and me pulling out of our driveway in the dark of the morning, heading for an all-day shopping trip to a tall girl shop somewhere. A knot came up in my throat and I swallowed hard. Mother always seemed to find time to take me, no matter how long the drive.

The woman interrupted my thoughts. "I wish my daughter could hang around with someone your size. If I've told her once, I've told her a thousand times not to pal around with short girls. They only make her look taller. Friends your size would make her look so much smaller."

I did not reply.

She continued. "It's a shame . . . a crying shame. She really could be a pretty girl if she just wasn't so tall. She just doesn't have much of a chance."

No, ma'am . . . she doesn't.

Plan Ahead

As my parents influenced me through example, I have tried with varying degrees of success to influence my own family and friends to have a sense of humor. There is little doubt in my mind that this effort to influence others has, in return, helped develop my own sense of humor.

Family and friends are the place to begin influencing others to have a sense of humor, but it does not stop here. Much of our social interaction takes place in work situations and with casual acquaintances. Trying to influence everyone with whom we interact to have a sense of humor is a challenge that will provide you with many rewards.

Since my profession requires a great deal of traveling, I have the opportunity to influence a large number of people that I'll probably see only once. Whether a person is a taxi driver, gate agent, bellman, or CEO of a large corporation, I try to practice what I preach and influence the folks I meet toward the humorous side of life. One of the best compliments I've ever received came through a fellow speaker, Larry Moles from Lima, Ohio. Larry called me after a trip he made to Charleston, South Carolina. During a taxi ride in Charleston, he mentioned to the driver that he was a professional speaker. The driver then told him that he had another professional speaker in his cab the previous summer—a very tall, funny lady. Larry mentioned my name and the driver not only remembered that was correct, but told Larry of something humorous I said during the trip. "He started laughing when he told me about it," Larry said when he called to tell me of the incident. I knew my efforts were worth it. Most of all, it made me more determined to continue to try to influence others in this direction.

The Funny Skies

It is also a good practice to observe closely people who appear to be successful in maintaining their humor because they are usually successful in influencing others to do the same. Observing their successes help to make my day and further develop my own sense of humor. I have found that one of the best places for me to make these observations is—of all places—the airline industry.

There are always exceptions, of course, but as a whole, airline personnel make up a group that knows the value of influencing people to keep a sense of humor. Because I fly so many days a month, I'm very familiar with the attitudes these people frequently encounter with their customers—the flying public. I enjoy watching gate and counter agents, pilots, and especially the flight attendants, to see what makes some of them successful at keeping their humor intact while others are not. I have concluded that the successful ones are the ones who have developed the habit of influencing the passengers to keep a sense of humor, which in most cases, enables them to keep their own. It may be a survival technique for them. For me, it is further proof that making it a priority to influence those around us to develop a sense of humor only serves to enhance our own humor. Let me share a few examples from the hundreds of times I have noticed this humor theory in practice.

But first, to better understand the value of these seemingly simple statements used to influence others, picture crowded planes, disgruntled passengers, and mothers traveling with small children screaming at the top of their lungs because their ears are popping. Visualize overhead bins crammed to the brink with suitcases that should have been checked, hanging bags weighing over twenty pounds, and three large-size passengers who do not know each other jammed side by side in three seats suitable for elementary school children. Close your eyes and imagine several hundred people who are all afraid they have missed their connections trying to lug carry-on bags up a small aisle as quickly as possible. Realize that many of these people, who would not dream of causing problems in other situations, seem to suddenly snap at airline personnel and blame them for their current plights.

Now picture how the reactions to the influencing statements listed below helped everyone involved:

Situation: 6:00 A.M. flight. Most of the passengers probably got up around 3:30 or 4:00 A.M. to get to the airport to check in by 5:30. It's cold. Dark. Babies are crying, and the pilot who also arose very early, says:

"Good morning, ladies and gentlemen, boys and girls. We're glad you're with us for this flight to Milwaukee. Your pilot and copilot are old, but extremely reliable. Your flight attendants are young, pretty and will attend to your needs. If you have any problems during the flight, let us know right then, because we do not permit grumbling and mumbling as you leave the plane."

Situation: The same as above, but a different pilot. Flying out of Atlanta.

"Good morning, folks. We're just about under way for our flight from Atlanta to New York City. We've just talked to the people up there and thought you might be interested. It's a clear day in the Big Apple, with a temperature of . . . 13 degrees. NOW would be a good time to ask yourself if you really need to go to New York City?"

Situation: Again, early morning.

As I sat on a United flight waiting to depart Greensboro, a flight attendant walked up the aisle, turning from side to side saying to sleepy passengers, "Blanket or pillow? Blanket or pillow?" A few seconds later, a second attendant walked along the same path saying, "Magazine or newspaper? Magazine or newspaper?" After they passed, a third attendant, grinning from ear to ear, came up the aisle singing out "Hugs or kisses? Hugs or kisses?"

It just started the day off right for everyone.

Situation: Big airport. Huge jumbo jets everywhere. A small commuter inches its way to a runway.

A hush fell over the passengers on the small commuter plane as it taxied away from the terminal to line up for takeoff from La Guardia Airport. We could not help but notice the massive jumbo jets all around us. It was eerie to look straight out our windows into the wheels of huge carriers.

Apparently, the pilot knew the passengers might be apprehensive about being the smallest kid on the block. As we slowly crept along he announced, "Ladies and gentleman. You'll notice we are methodically inching our way to the runway. Air Traffic Control doesn't have an exact sequence . . . but it's just like driving on the freeway. SOMEBODY will let us little guys in. They ALWAYS do."

Situation: Bumpy flight. The flight attendants may have to stop serving drinks. Very few people have been served.

Flight attendant: "Ladies and gentlemen. The pilot has notified us it looks a little bumpy ahead. We are going to continue cabin service as long as possible, but we may have to stop." (A moan goes through the passengers who have not been served.) The flight attendant adds, "Those of you who already have drinks may want to hold them . . . over your neighbor's lap."

The moaners and groaners grinned.

Situation: Any flight, passengers exiting the plane. Passengers always try to stand up in the aisles before the plane has come to a complete stop. Not only is the seat belt sign usually on, the flight attendants are always reminding them to "remain seated."

On a late flight into Los Angeles we were held out on the runway after we landed. The plane had come to a complete stop, but we were a long way from the gate. Before people could stand up, one of the female attendants came on the P.A. system and said, "Ladies and gentleman, please look into the center aisle. You'll see one of our macho male flight attendants walking toward the front of the plane." (A young man walking up the aisle smiled and waved to the passengers as though he was in a parade.)

"Notice his muscles." (He flexed.) "If any of you stand up before we come to a complete stop at the gate . . . he'll PUSH YOU DOWN." Everyone laughed, and, of course, all eyes were on this guy as he walked along. Suddenly he made a quick turn and with a smile on his face shouted at one of the passengers, "AND KEEP QUIET!" Everybody broke into even greater laughter, especially a man across the aisle from where this had taken place. Just as suddenly and still smiling, the attendant wheeled around to this man and said, "AND TAKE OFF YOUR HAT!"

People were still laughing when they walked off the plane.

Situation: Flight attendant, again trying to keep people seated.

A few minutes after landing, while taxiing up to the gate the flight attendant casually announces to the delight of the passengers: "Ladies and Gentlemen, our pilots are both former New York cab drivers. I point that out now that we are out of the air and they are driving us up to the gate. Please remain seated—for your own safety—until they get us to the gate. At that time, you will be able to gather your belongings and . . . TRAMPLE OTHERS AS YOU TRY TO BE THE FIRST OFF THE PLANE!"

Situation: Again, trying to get passengers to stay in their seats.

As we taxied out to the runway for a cross-country flight, six businessmen traveling together began to switch seats at the same time. All six of them just stood up and started changing places and swapping brief cases. I could see the flight attendant, who was strapped in her seat, watching them as she shook her head in disgust. She reached for the public address system, and I expected her to emphatically command that they be seated. She got her results another way, and probably kept down her own stress level.

With a smile on her face, she said, "Gentleman, when the music stops, find a seat." All the passengers burst out laughing. The six men, scrambling like little boys playing musical chairs, hurriedly sat back down.

Situation: And one last time, attempting to keep passengers in their seats during taxiing.

As the flight was still pulling into a gate at the Raleigh/ Durham Airport, passengers began to stand and gather their belongings. The flight attendant clicked on the P.A. system and politely announced with a smile, "Ladies and gentlemen, those of you standing at this time should have a GOOD VIEW of the fasten seat belt sign."

Situation: The plane slowly makes a turn and the passengers realize we've been put in a holding pattern.

Pilot: "We're experiencing a slight delay and we're going to hold for a little while. It's nothing to worry about. They're turning the airport around, and we're going to wait up here till they get it ju-st right for us. Now, doesn't that make you feel better?"

Situation: Overbearing male passenger traveling with a group of his friends. He thinks he's a prize.

Mr. Cool, in a loud voice said to a female flight attendant as she served him dinner, "Honey, do you fool around?"

I know a thousand good put-downs must have raced through her mind, but she seemed determined to keep her sense of humor and politely answered, "I have a boy friend."

The guy, mostly for the benefit of his friends, said, "So what? My girl friend fools around on me."

Again, her humor influenced the tone of the situation. She turned and looked him straight in the eyes, smiled and said, "I can certainly understand why."

His friends roared as she smiled sweetly and moved up the aisle. The instigator even shook his head and grinned. The magic came when she said it with a smile.

Situation: An unexpected jolt in the air.

I was on a commuter flight coming into Detroit from Lansing, Michigan. The weather was clear, the flight smooth. Suddenly we hit an air pocket and were bumped high off our seats. People began to nervously look at each other. It was very reassuring when the flight attendant clicked on the public address system and in a deep voice calmly and slowly said one sentence without any further explanation. "There—is—nothing—to—worry—about."

People looked around at each other and smiled. We all felt better. I glanced at her in the back of the plane. She was grinning from ear to ear.

Situation: Routine flight, late in the day. Tired passengers.

Flight attendant over P.A. system: "Ladies and gentlemen, we will be landing in St. Louis in just a few minutes. Prior to landing, we will be coming through the cabin and will be politely snatching any cups that you have left at this point. DO NOT GET IN OUR WAY! WE ARE VICIOUS!"

A ripple of laughter moved through the plane.

Situation: Possible mounting passenger anger.

I was on a packed—and delayed—flight waiting to leave out of Atlanta. As the flight attendant passed up the aisle, a passenger asked, "How long will it be before we leave?"

She leaned toward the man and under her breath, whispered,

"The pilots are not here yet." The man boomed, "THE PILOTS ARE NOT HERE YET?" Everybody put down their papers and began to shift their weight back and forth in their seats.

She smiled sweetly at the questioning passenger and answered loud enough for those seated in the vicinity to hear, "If you want us to, the flight attendants can fly the plane. The truth is, there are only three buttons in the cockpit that really count—the on and off, the up and down, and the stop and go. The rest of the buttons are for show to justify their big salaries."

Everyone chuckled and relaxed.

Situation: Mother with her hands full. Little boy passenger on his first flight.

We were still on the ground when the excited little boy rang his call button and summoned the flight attendant, "When do we get the drinks?"

She said, "I can't serve drinks until we are in the air." His face fell; and his mother, holding his squirming baby sister, attempted to divert his attention to a magazine.

The flight attendant's eyes suddenly lit up as though she had a brainstorm, and she said, "But you can go see the bathroom now if you want to." The little boy proceeded quickly up the aisle, having totally forgotten it would be a while until he could get a drink. The baby sister continued to squirm, but the mother and other passengers smiled.

Situation: Anxious passengers. All trying to hurry through security to their flights.

On a Sunday morning in late September, I was flying from Pittsburgh to Greensboro. I had gone to the airport early in order to miss the traffic for the winless Steelers vs. Houston Oilers game that day. The fog was thick and I suspected the flights were grounded. I was correct. The airport was already packed with passengers in various stages of grumbling.

People pretended to look off in the distance as they tried to inch their way in front of others at security. They thought they were clever, but they were still breaking in line. Tension filled the air. As I put my bags on the conveyer belt, I asked one of the guards, "Is the fog holding up most of the flights?" The woman quickly answered, "I don't know about the flights—but boy are we glad to get this fog! The Steelers might win a game if the other team can't see them."

Everyone within hearing burst out laughing, and they did not seem to be quite as impolite after that.

Situation: Plane about to land.

Pilot on Delta flight arriving in Dallas: "You may be interested to know our touchdown speed here in Dallas will be 135 miles per hour . . . which is similar to the speed of my teenage son pulling into our driveway."

Situation: Bad weather, but a perfect landing.

The pilot after bringing down a big L1011 smoothly and on time, cut on the public address system and in a slow, mechanical voice announced, "ONCE AGAIN, SCIENCE TRIUMPHS OVER MYTH AND SUPERSTITION."

Situation: Competitors on the same flight.

Jerry and I were on a Delta flight from Orlando to Atlanta on Super Bowl Sunday, 1985. The Bears and the Patriots were playing for the championship. Midway in the flight, the pilot announced, "Ladies and Gentlemen. I know you're interested in what's happening at the Super Bowl. For you Chicago fans, the score at the half is 23-3 in favor of your beloved Bears.

For you Patriot fans . . . there's a good view of Jacksonville on your right."

Situation: Early morning flight. Passengers on the edge of their seats waiting for coffee. The flight attendant knows a secret and says:

"Ladies and gentlemen, each of you has an important decision to make and it could influence the rest of your day. Apparently, at a previous stop, the ground crew had trouble flushing out the water tank in our kitchen, which means a little detergent was left in the water. We will be happy to serve you coffee or tea, but any drink made with water is going to remind you of your mother washing your mouth out with soap. If you've been a bad boy or girl, you may decide you need that. It's up to you."

With that she put down the public address microphone, walked to the passengers in row one, and in a cheery voice asked, "And now . . . may I get you a cup of coffee?"

Passengers who would have been upset at not receiving morning coffee, laughed.

Situation: A very crowded airport. Passengers hurrying from gate to gate, bumping into each other. There is a steady monotone of routine airport announcements such as: "Mr. So-and-So. Mr. So-and-So, please go to your nearest paging phone" and "Mrs. John Doe, please report to the Delta ticket counter." No one seems to acknowledge hearing a single announcement until an unknown agent announces in a pleading voice:

"Attention, every person in the airport! Will the party meeting the six-year-old triplets PLEEEASE COME TO GATE 17!"

All within my sight burst out laughing.

The Big Rat

Of course, people in the airline industry are not successful with influencing all people to have a sense of humor, nor are they always successful at maintaining their own humor. Neither can we be completely successful. The important thing is that we continue to make the effort and not let the negative attitudes of others rub off on us. In fact, often it is the occasions in which we are unsuccessful in influencing others to have a sense of humor that provide us with good stories to share with others. For example . . .

I was in the process of renting an apartment in Durham, North Carolina, and quickly surmised that there must have been many more people needing apartments than space available. The man I was dealing with acted as though he was doing me a favor to even talk to me about it. After I said I wanted the apartment, he began to go over the rules.

"You can't put any nails in our apartments."

"Yes sir."

"And no tape on the walls . . . anywhere."

"I understand."

"Be careful where you put your plants."

"Yes sir."

"It will probably be better not to have any plants inside at all."

No comment.

Every time I asked a question, he acted as though it was ridiculous. I knew he had been through this many times before, but come on . . . I began to think, "I'm going to get through to this man somehow."

Finally, he said, "And one more thing. Do you have any pets?" Before I could even respond, he interrupted. "We DO NOT ALLOW pets if they weigh over twenty pounds. No sir. NO PETS over twenty pounds!"

"Well, I will be all right there," I said. Then, trying to establish some type of normal rapport with this future landlord, I added tongue-in-cheek, "My son has a white mouse. Do I have to get rid of that?"

Mr. Personality slammed his pencil down on his desk and

looked at me condescendingly, "Lady, if it is alive, and it is over twenty pounds, you will HAVE to get rid of it. And IF . . . YOU . . . DON'T, and I find out about it? Well, I'LL GET RID OF IT FOR YOU!"

With the thought of a twenty pound white mouse coming to mind, I leaned forward and looked the man right in the eyes. "I'll tell you what. If that mouse gets up to nineteen pounds, I'll get rid of it BEFORE you tell me to."

He never cracked a smile.

Too Pompous to Pop

I am reminded of another time my efforts did not work. I was seated on a plane in an aisle seat when a man boarded the plane. He obviously thought he was the most important person on the trip. He swept down the aisle, clutching his brief case and scowling slightly at anyone presumptuous enough to be in his way. His suit was flawlessly tailored, his cologne impressive, and his nails buffed to a discreet shine. Flight attendants snapped to attention, and little old ladies fluttered like chickens to get out of his way.

When he reached my row, he checked his ticket and inhaled sharply. "Why," he demanded of a flight attendant, "do I have a window seat when I specifically requested an aisle seat?" He stared at the seat next to me as if it were an open sewage pit.

The flight attendant made soothing sounds, but Mr. Big had waited until the last minute for his dramatic entrance. The crowded plane was about to take off and there was no time to shuffle the seating arrangements. The thought crossed my mind to let him have my seat, but it was a long flight and I wanted an aisle seat because I want to take my legs with me.

Before I could stand up to let him in, he climbed over me to the window seat. I smiled in polite sympathy and said something like, "There's not much room is there?" He said loudly to the air around us, "I have a lot of work to do, so I don't want to talk."

For an instant I hesitated. Then I put my thumbs in my ears—fingers wiggling—stuck out my tongue, and made a sound that is sometimes called a Bronx cheer.

I would like to tell you the man broke into a big smile because I influenced him to keep his sense of humor. In fact, he moved to the back of the plane.

But the flight attendant gave me a bottle of wine.

The Smile

Well, of course, there are always going to be those individuals who have built a wall around them that is so humor proof it will be difficult to break through. But as surely as we can learn to develop a sense of humor, in most cases so can we influence those around us to develop a sense of humor. And always remember that on the occasions when our efforts to influence others do not work, we do have one valuable alternative remaining . . . the smile!

Keep Smiling

There was no doubt about it. The stage was slanted, not just a little slanted . . . very slanted. It was so slanted that there were four steps to the stage on one side, three on the other.

The old elementary school auditorium was the site of a high school beauty pageant that I was emceeing a few years ago. The people in this small Alabama town were accustomed to the slant. Stage hands knew to put bricks on one side of all the props so that they would not slide. When people in the audience sat down, they just automatically tilted to their right and stayed tilted for the rest of the evening. They no longer thought about it, but when I walked on stage, I felt like I was on a sinking ship.

The lectern on the stage was missing one side, but the stage-hands just turned it a little more toward the wall. The footlights were light bulbs from home. If people were involved in the event, they brought some bulbs. When it was over, they came down front, unscrewed their bulbs, and took them home. You get the picture. Small town America, God love it.

However, the enthusiasm was high and the contestants were excited and nervous. One of my duties as mistress of ceremonies, I believed, was to influence them to stay calm. I told them my philosophy about the importance of smiling: "No matter what happens, keep a smile on your face. If something goes wrong, the audience will tighten up because they want you to do well. If you smile, you can influence everyone else to relax. They will think you have everything under control."

One of the contestants—I'll call her Louisa—said, "That's easy for you to say, Jeanne. You did comedy for your talent in the Miss America Pageant, but I play the piano." I didn't have the heart to tell her I had not done comedy. I was singing and playing the ukulele the best I could. People just thought it was comedy.

"No," I told them, "it doesn't matter what you are doing. If something goes wrong, keep smiling. People may never guess there is a problem. If they do, I guarantee that you can influence them to smile with you."

When it was time for Louisa's performance in the talent competition, the stagehands rolled the piano out on stage and put it carefully on the X-marks that had been put down with masking tape on the floor. There was, however, one small problem. The stage crew forgot to put the bricks behind the wheels of the piano! It was situated virtually on a downhill slant.

I introduced Louisa, and it was evident she was scared to death, but she was smiling. She walked out on stage, stood next to the piano, and smiled from ear to ear before she sat down.

Unfortunately, she was not playing a soft, slow melody. No, indeed. Her mama and daddy—seated in the second row, tilting to the right, of course—had paid for eleven years of piano lessons, and she was going to show what she had learned. When she started playing, she hit the keys with all her might: DA DA DA

DUMMMM! And the piano rolled. Let me repeat; the piano rolled! The audience gasped and watched in horror. They were so taken back that they almost stopped tilting.

You would have been so proud of her. Her face registered shock, but she kept on playing as she slowly turned to the audience and—bless her little heart—smiled. Everyone breathed a sigh of relief.

From that point on, a spectacle unfolded before an auditorium full of hometown folks that will never be forgotten. It could have been tragic, but Louisa was smiling so hard that it became hilarious. The more she played, the more the piano rolled away from her. People sat goggle-eyed. It didn't scoot away from her, but it rolled jerkingly depending on the intensity of her playing. At one point, just to reach the keys, she had to stretch her little arms straight out in front of her, and when she did, she again looked out and smiled. Actually, by then a chisel could not have made a dent in her lips.

When the time came that she could barely reach the keys, I thought "Oh, it's all over now." But she just kept playing with her left hand while she reached down by her knees with her right hand and scooted the bench closer to the keys. As she did, she turned and smiiilllled. She was working magic. The audience burst into applause.

As her presentation progressed, she pursued that piano roll-by-roll across the stage while the people cheered and Jaycees raced frantically behind the curtain trying to decide what to do. I could see them mouthing words at each other as they threw their arms around in the air and began to corner the stagehand who had blown the assignment. About a minute into her three-minute piece, they made a decision. I watched from my side of the stage in disbelief as the stagehand held culpable picked up a large cement block, hunched over, and began to tiptoe out on the stage toward the piano. (Why do people think that if they tiptoe, others will not see them?)

The sight of this huge man, lugging a big cement block and tiptoeing his way toward the piano, brought gales of laughter from the audience—attention that he seemed to enjoy. He had almost made it to the piano when Louisa—still smiling and still playing—suddenly snapped her head from the judges to his direction and began to glare at him from behind her fixed smile. Her quick steely-eyed stare caused him to come to a complete stop at the piano, and when their eyes met, the people in the audience immediately grew quiet, their eyes fixed on the scenario on stage. Louisa was like a cat stalking her prey. She never missed a note in her Etude, and she never blinked as she glared at the Jaycee who slooooowly turned and tiptoed off the stage . . . taking the cement block with him.

Through it all, Louisa kept playing and smiling, and the piano kept rolling slowly, inch by inch. By the time she finished her number a minute later, she and the piano, as well as the Jaycee and cement block, were in the wings. Pandemonium swept through the crowd as they rose to their feet, cheering and clapping.

It took a few minutes for the commotion and the buzz of conversation to stop. When things finally quietened, I introduced the next contestant, a piccolo player who took her place on stage and then swayed sharply to the left in order to look the audience straight in the eyes.

I rushed backstage to find Louisa. I did not have to look far. She was coming around the back curtain and making a bee-line straight toward me.

"Where's the piano?" I gasped.

And this sixteen-year-old girl, still smiling, said through gritted teeth, "When I bailed out, it was heading toward Montgomery."

Then she grabbed me by the arms and said, "But I never stopped smiling. Do you think anybody suspected anything was wrong?" We both collapsed, laughing so hard we couldn't speak.

It's Your Turn to Work Magic

Begin in the home by influencing your spouse and children to develop a sense of humor, then influence your neighbors, friends and co-workers. But don't stop here. Make an effort to influence every person with whom you interact. This will be a great challenge, but will provide many rewards.

Also observe particular groups of people who appear to you to be successful in maintaining their sense of humor. I have found that in my lifestyle the airline industry is a great place for me to make these observations. Observe in your lifestyle groups who appear to you to be successful, and learn from their successes.

Finally, realize that although your attempts to influence everyone you meet to have a sense of humor may not be successful, the process will continue to benefit your own sense of humor. And remember, when your efforts are not successful, you have one valuable alternative remaining . . . the smile.

Potion 6
See the Humor in Stressful, Awkward, or Unpleasant Situations

I t is important to have a good sense of humor in mundane, everyday situations and when everything is going well. But it is equally desirable to maintain a humorous attitude in stressful, awkward, or unpleasant situations. We accept the fact that these kinds of situations will sometimes arise when as few as two individuals are interacting. An indefinitely great number of books, cassettes, and seminars offer alternative ways of preventing stress. Of course, psychiatrists treat mental disorders that occasionally develop from stressful situations, but of all the suggestions made by these sources, humor may provide the best medicine for preventing potential unpleasantries. Whenever we are able to see the humorous side of a tense situation, many times the situation ceases to exist. Making a determined effort to see the humor in all aspects of life, the bad as well as the good, is also essential for developing a good sense of humor.

How do we use humor to ease the stresses of life? Does this apply if you are the person you believe to have been wronged? Yes, it applies most especially when we think we have been wronged, and you will find that asking yourself the following questions will prove valuable in seeing the humor in unpleasant situations.

1. *Can I provide a humor cue that will relieve tension and not provide stress for someone else?*

   I'm a strong believer in giving humor cues to yourself and to the people around you. People pick up on cues . . . and run with them. Watch people the next time a tense situation occurs in your family or in your work place. In many cases, people stand around, waiting on a cue from someone as to how they will all react to the tense situation. If someone gets angry, many times everyone will get upset and eventually angry. If someone falls apart, they might all fall apart, but if one person . . . maybe you . . . can see the humor in what has happened and make the most of it, people will pick up on that cue quickly and the tone will be set. The problem may be prevented altogether or handled in a few minutes. The important thing is to see the humor in the situation and make the most of it.

2. *Will this be funny when I tell about it later? Is this the funny thing I am going to find today in my everyday situation? Is it something for my humor collection?*

   I realize I am a humorous speaker, and I am always looking for material for presentations; and when something unpleasant occurs, I immediately start thinking about how I will tell about it later. How can I stretch it a little? What are the funny lines everybody will be saying about this event as the day progresses? What I have really found in approaching these situations in this manner is that I am less prone to get upset myself. The individual determined to develop a better sense of humor will get the same results.

3. *How would this situation appear if I were not directly involved?*
When something unpleasant begins to occur, mentally take
yourself out of the arena. Think about how the entire event
would play as a thirty-minute situation comedy on television.
How would the fool of the show react? The problem solver? The
star? In most instances, while we are analyzing the situation,
the tension will pass. If not, our frame of mind changes so that
we will not react with anger, but with a smile.

Now, examine several examples where humor was used to ease
what could have been tense, awkward, or unpleasant situations.

A Good Turn

I travel a lot. Several years ago, I got ready to leave and my
husband said, "Do you THINK it would be possible—BEFORE
you leave today—to wash a load of clothes. We have not had
clean underwear in THREE days."

Now here was a potentially tense situation because I did not
even have time to stuff those clothes into the machine. I did
not want to snap at him and leave on an unpleasant note. So I
decided to see the humor in it and make the most of it.

I gave him my biggest smile and said, "A smart man like
you! You have your Ed.D. Surely you are smart enough to know
you can turn your underwear inside out, and it is good for
THREE MORE DAYS!"

The Challenge of Parenting

The greatest challenge that I—or most parents for that matter—
have in seeing the humor in tense situations is dealing with the
antics of our children; in my case, my son Beaver.

I guess it would have been unrealistic to expect a boy growing up in a home with two adults who place a high priority on
humor to do exactly what those adults would choose for him to

do and conform to their expectations in an orderly, organized manner. Looking back, I might wonder if the fact I gathered humorous speech material from his exploits only served to "egg Beaver on." Actually, I do not believe that to be the case. After going with my friends through the childhood and teenage years of their children, I believe all parents find some of the deeds of our offspring to be, at times, unbelievable. I expect it was the same for my parents with me. But for the past several years, that has not been my concern. What has been my concern was to see the humor in some pretty stressful situations involving my own child—situations that in the long run proved harmless, such as:

. . . **"PERSON," the HAMSTER.** When Beaver was in the third grade, he asked me to go in the backyard late one afternoon and see where he and his friends had buried "Person," the hamster. (If a family has a little boy named "Beaver," it only stands to reason that they will have a hamster named "Person.") As we looked down at the little rocks and flowers of the newly made grave, Beaver broke the silence of the moment by saying, "He was barely breathing when we threw the dirt on top of him."

. . . **HAVING TWO REPORT CARDS in the NINTH GRADE.** Somehow—"mysteriously," of course—Beaver wound up with two report cards in the ninth grade. One card was for Jerry and me to review and sign. It was made out by ninth-grade girls and generally contained "A's" with a "B" or two scattered in to keep things believable. The second card was filled in by teachers, and needless to say, the grades were a bit lower. This little scheme went undetected until two weeks before the end of the year when a teacher called to say Beaver was failing math for the grading period. I suggested it was a little late to be calling when the boy had made straight "A's" in math until that point. The stunned silence on the other end of the telephone was my first clue.

. . . **THE SCHOOL PLAY RUSE.** At one point, Beaver and several friends were being punished by their teacher by having to stay after school every afternoon for two weeks. Of course, he told me that the reason he was staying after school was that he had gotten the lead in a school play and he was rehearsing. I was so proud. SO PROUD, in fact, that after a week I dropped by the school to offer to help with the props and costumes. "The props," I explained patiently to the school secretary. "You know, the props for the BIG school play."

. . . THE SECOND STORY HOIST. During the tenth grade, Beaver was grounded one weekend. He kept calling us where we were playing bridge, asking an odd assortment of questions such as "What pan do I use to cook popcorn?" He called so often that we became suspicious. Jerry went home and found Beaver was not there. Evidently, he had been calling us from various points around town to keep us from calling him. Jerry locked the house, hid the usual keys, and returned to the bridge game. When we came back home around 11:30 P.M., the car lights shone on four of Beaver's friends attempting to hoist him through a very high, second level window.

. . . THE CAMOUFLAGED CAR. The week before high school graduation, Beaver and nine of his friends painted his car "camouflage." They called it camouflage, but along with the greens and browns, it also had a number of yellow and white splotches. Very concealing. When he ran out of gas at the beach the next week, they left the car on the side of the road and COULD NOT BE-LIEVE the police towed it away. "We don't know how they saw it, being camouflaged and all."

. . . THE RED PORSCHE. Beaver and his fraternity brothers left his car—with camouflage sandblasted off and painted over—on side of the road when it again ran out of gas. They were AMAZED to discover it was gone the next day. Unbeknownst to them, it had been towed away by the Virginia Highway Patrol—a fact we learned when they contacted us seventeen days later by letter. Jerry promptly called Beaver and told him we were going to buy him a red Porsche because he was doing so well in school. That should have been his clue that this was not so. But no, Beaver was ecstatic! After a few minutes of euphoria, Jerry added, "We'll come up tomorrow and get your car to trade in on it," know-

ing the boy had no idea where the car was. "Uh . . . Uh . . . ,"
Beaver stammered. "There is a slight problem with that. I'm not
sure where the car is." Jerry said, "We are. It is with the Virginia
Highway Patrol." There was a looooong pause, and Beaver finally
said, "And I guess this means . . . there's no red Porsche?"

   . . . **THE WORD SPREADS.** Then there was the time
Jerry and I checked into a hotel in Beaver's college town, and the
student desk clerk asked if we had a son or daughter at the nearby
school. When we told her we had a son, named Beaver, she burst
out laughing and then became embarrassed. "I'm sorry," she said,
"but I know him . . . and I've just never thought about Beaver
having parents."

Red Ryder and Faithful Side-Kick

The name Beaver? Let me make one thing clear. I did not name
my child Beaver. College friends started calling him that when
he was born, and it stuck. If you think he was named after the
television show "Leave it to Beaver" you can consider yourself a
fairly young person. If you remember Red Ryder and his faithful
side-kick, Little Beaver, you are in my age range and know where
he got his nickname. Now that little baby is almost 6 feet, eight
inches tall, weighs 230 pounds and is still called . . . Beaver.

   We told him when he went to college it would be a good time
to forget his nickname and become known by his real name. "No
way," he said. "I like having a name that is different. People
remember it." I did not have the heart to tell him I had recently
run into a friend whom I had known in college and after a few
minutes of conversation, she said, "And tell me, how is Rooster?"

   Anyway, Beaver it is, and shall remain for his mother. I am
sure by now, I could never call him anything else.

   There is a time in every person's life—I believe it is when
we are about eight or nine years old—when our teeth are pro-
portionally large compared to our head. We all go through that
period. When Beaver was that age, not only were his teeth very

large, but the front ones angled in different directions. It took years of braces to get them straightened . . . just in time to catch a few elbows to the mouth in high school basketball.

Once during that big teeth period of Beaver's life, we went into a restaurant, and of course, I am like most mothers—I give directions. "Put your coat on that hook, Beaver." "Sit in that chair, Beaver." "Here's the menu. What do you want to order, Beaver?"

All of the sudden, a woman at the next table GRABBED me by the arm and said, "How would YOU like it, if he called you GIRAFFE?"

Frank Caller

Even though I may be six feet, two inches tall, weigh 160 pounds, and wear a size 11B shoe, I never refer to my size as "big." I prefer words such as "stately" and "statuesque," and let us not forget "willowy." But I have told my family for years not to refer to me as "big."

Therefore, one can imagine how I felt once when we were keeping my sister's child, Jeanne, named after me. The telephone rang and Beaver picked it up. The man on the other end said, "May I speak to Jeanne?" And the boy whom I had fed and clothed for so many years said, "Do you want to speak to little Jeanne . . . or BIIGGGG Jeanne?"

The man said, "If there is one there BIGGER than the one I know, I don't want to speak to anybody!"

Bewildered Shoppers

It was Christmas and my husband and son were at the local department store considering a blouse as a gift for me. Naturally, the sales lady asked, "What size blouse does your wife wear?"

Jerry and Beaver looked at each other and shrugged their shoulders. "I have no idea," Jerry answered.

"Well, what size foundation does she wear?" the clerk continued patiently.

Beaver's eyes lit up. "Eleven B," he said proudly.

. . . and he was soooooo close.

Questionable Information

It doesn't matter if you live in North Carolina, Massachusetts, or Timbuktu. After children learn to write, they all get those forms to fill out on the first day of school. The teacher instructs, "Write down your parents' names and occupations."

Next to mother's name, Beaver wrote "Jeanne Robertson." One would expect him to get that correct in junior high school.

Next to occupation, he wrote "works conventions." Then he penciled in . . . "and gets paid by the night."

Just Following Directions

Mothers, are mothers, are mothers. The area of the country in which one lives does not matter at all. Motherhood transcends regional differences.

At a banquet in Flint, Michigan, a mother made an instant ally in me when I asked if she had any children. "Yes," she said. "A sixteen year-old son."

I thought about Beaver and asked, "Is he staying with friends this weekend?"

"No," she replied. "He's here with us . . . at that first table right there." I looked out in the audience at the good-looking young man. Neither of us spoke for a few seconds and then she sighed and said, "We were afraid to leave him at home alone."

"I understand," I said, and we just looked at each other and nodded. I thought about the time we left Beaver at home for a week.

When Beaver was nineteen . . . my husband and I wanted

to attend the National Speakers Association convention in Washington. Beaver had always gone to the conventions with us. But this particular year, he wanted to stay home by himself for a week.

We knew this could be trouble, but he was nineteen, and was scheduled to work at a nearby basketball camp. He swore to us he could handle anything that happened, so we agreed he could stay. Of course, we set down the rules.

"When we get back," I said, "I want this house to be clean, just like we left it." (Beaver wanted to know if that meant I would clean it BEFORE I left. Cute.)

My husband added, "And I don't want more than five people IN THIS HOUSE at any one time . . . but always, more than two."

I said, "I don't want any girls IN THIS HOUSE, period."

"And furthermore," we added, there will be no drinking IN THIS HOUSE while we are gone."

The neighbors said . . . it was the LARGEST YARD PARTY they had ever seen.

The Pangs of Motherhood

After a luncheon speech in Washington, D.C., I hurried to the airport and made an earlier connection home. This put me in Burlington an hour and a half earlier than expected. Arriving home earlier than expected often leads to interesting situations as far as children are concerned.

Walking toward the back door from the car, I heard kids' voices in the house. On the back porch, I shouted, "Beaver, I'm home."

Silence.

Entering the kitchen, I yelled, "Beaver, it's Mom. I'm home early."

Nothing.

"O.K. I know you're hiding. I heard you when I came on the porch." I glanced into the den and then went upstairs toward the bedrooms on the second level of the house. "O.K. Wherever you are, I'm not going to look for you. I'm tired."

From the very small bathroom off the back of the upstairs master bedroom, literally the "last corner" of the house, I heard Beaver's voice. "I'm in here, Mom. I'll be out in a minute."

I headed back down the stairs and a thought hit me. Call it mother's instinct. I knew that something was not right. I had heard voices as in "more than one" when I came up on the porch. Like a homing pigeon, without breaking stride, I turned and headed back up the stairs.

"Beaver, what are you doing in there?"

"I'll be out in a minute, Mom. My stomach's a little upset."

Mother's instinct went into overtime. There are always a horde of little boys around our house, but I had never known them to go into the bathroom together.

"Beaver, are you in there by yourself?"

A loooooong pause. Shuffling behind the door. Finally, "No ma'am."

The door opened slowly. Standing on the commode was one of the cutest little girls you would ever want to see. Her eyes were as big as salad plates; big tears were streaming down her face.

Non-parents will not understand my emotions. Parents of young people who have either passed through the teen years or are approaching the teen years as Beaver was at this time will understand. A flash went through my body.

"Who are you?" was all I could muster, but my neck must have been turning red.

"Now wait a minute Mom; there's nothing wrong here. She rode the bus home with me. We were in the kitchen getting something to eat, and we heard you coming up. We knew we weren't supposed to be in the house, we ran up here and hid . . . and . . . here we are. But nothing's wrong. Nothing has HAPPENED."

The girl spoke. "It hasn't Mrs. Robertson. I promise." She was still standing on the commode seat.

Since the rule was, "No girls in the house if an adult is not home," parents can imagine my anger. Within four minutes the little girl was gone, Beaver was in his room, and I was trying to get under control.

I mention this because my immediate thought was what most working mothers think. "If I had been at home, this would not have happened."

I called Jerry immediately to relate the incident and announced that I was canceling all my speeches, explaining, "I need to be at home until Beaver grows up."

"Actually," Jerry said, "it's better that you travel. If you had not been working, you would have been playing tennis this afternoon and the situation would have been much worse."

"Worse?"

"You would have had a racquet in your hand when you found them."

Later that night after a long family discussion, I just had to ask Beaver one more question before we put the matter behind us. "By the way, son, what was she doing standing on the commode?"

"She was thinking about jumping out the window."

"Out of a high, SECOND STORY WINDOW? Surely you would not have let her do that?"

"Are you kidding? I was begging, 'JUMP . . . JUMP!'"

The Proper Equipment

In rearing children, it is very difficult to see humor in certain situations. Beaver's first experience at basketball camp was a severe test of my ability to see the humor in a very awkward situation.

The week before Beaver was to go to camp, I received a letter listing the items he should bring. One of the items was . . . "athletic supporter." I am not a fool. I knew they did not want him to bring a cheerleader with him to camp.

I more or less knew what an "athletic supporter" was, but having grown up with just sisters, I had never shopped for one before. Beaver was spending the week with his grandmother, and husband Jerry was out of town at a meeting. I put off making the purchase, hoping Jerry might come back a day early from his trip. Finally, late on Saturday afternoon, I had to make the purchase myself.

I am almost hesitant to even go into the buying of the thing. When I told the clerk what I wanted, he nodded and said, "What size?"

"I beg your pardon?"

"What size do you want?" he repeated.

"Size? I have no idea."

"Well, lady, I have to know an approximate size."

"Mister, the boy is nine years old. He has not let me see him undressed for two years."

Soon that clerk was replaced by another, and he said to me, "Look, Ma'am, we have to have a size or we're not going to be able to sell you the article."

"Oh, all right," I said in desperation. "I'll take a wild guess. No bigger than your little finger."

Two sales clerks later, I finally had my purchase.

Beaver came home from his grandmother's at 11:00 P.M. that night, and I sent him immediately to bed. Of course, I was up all night, washing and drying his clothes, but the next morning I had him ready to go.

Since it was a day camp, I was waiting in front of the nearby university gymnasium to pick him up that evening. When he came out walking toward the car as fast as he could, I knew something was wrong. I have never seen so many tears on one little boy in my entire life. Before he even got in the car he declared, "I'm NOT going back to that camp!"

I was still tired from doing the laundry all night, and I was not in the mood for this. "What in the world is wrong with you? Get in this car!"

"I mean it, Mama. I'm NOT COMING BACK to this camp."

"You WILL be here in the morning. "We can't get our money back."

He did not say anything for several miles; he just sat there, his bottom lip quivering. Finally he blurted out, "Why didn't you tell me about THAT THING?"

"Thing? What thing? What in the world are you talking about?"

"That thing you HID in my duffel bag. Right under the sandwiches."

Suddenly it dawned on me that he was talking about the athletic supporter. "Beaver, don't tell me you didn't know what that was."

"I didn't have any idea," he wailed.

"SURELY, some of the older boys told you."

"Yes, Ma'am. They TOLD ME all right. They said it was for a nosebleed, and put it on my nose, and wrapped it all 'round my head!"

Of course, any mother would have said the same thing I said: "Son, you don't have to go back to that camp tomorrow."

But he did have to go back. And the following Friday, on "come see your little boy play" day, Jerry and I had to go into that gymnasium and meet the coaches who just a few days earlier told our son, "Get back in the dressing room, and take that thing off your nose!"

I admit that it was not easy to see the humor in this particular awkward situation. However, I do know that a continuous effort to see humor in every situation—the bad as well as the good—definitely increases the joy of bringing up children.

Pungent and Malodorous

One speaking situation that leaves a particularly "poignant" impression on my memory is the night I spoke in Hereford, Texas. Hereford is a town that is literally built up around their stockyards, with the railroad tracks running right through downtown. Thousands of head of cattle from all over Texas and Oklahoma arrive in Hereford by rail on a daily basis and are held for auction in open air stockyards. Needless to say, the manure odor permeates the air for miles around.

I noticed the distinct odor as I drove into Hereford and checked into the motel. I did not mention it until my host picked me up and drove me to the country club, which is located several miles from the stockyards. As we got out of the automobile, the odor seemed to sock me in the face. I stood by the car a few seconds and then said, "Excuse me, but I need to get my breath."

My contact grinned. "Yea, it's pretty bad when the wind is blowing this way."

"Does the wind make that much difference?"

"Nope, but it makes conversation."

The fellow seemed amiable enough and it turned out he could see the humor in this situation. I just had to ask, "Do you ever get accustomed to the smell?"

"To tell you the truth, ma'am, when I leave town, I miss it."

"Oh, come on."

"Yep. I've lived in Hereford all my life."

Well, the folks in Hereford were great and I would go back

any time, but I remember thinking when I left, "I won't ever again speak with an odor such as that in the air."

Wrong.

A couple of years later, I arrived in Raleigh, to speak to the North Carolina School Food people. It was a large group with around twelve hundred expected for the banquet. When I arrived the ladies in charge were upset. It seemed that government officials in Raleigh had selected that afternoon to fertilize the grounds, and had completely covered the area around the convention center with cow manure. It was a once a year job, if that often. I knew from my Hereford trip that the smell of cow manure knows no boundaries. Sure enough, it reached the banquet room, and to say the least, it was the main topic of conversation.

The convention chairperson greeted me with, "Have you EVER smelled anything this bad in your life?" I wanted to say, "Lady, you oughta go to Hereford, Texas," but I figured she did not care at that point. As people will do, however, she took it all in stride and saw the humor in the pungent situation. In just a few minutes, she began her opening remarks with, "I have always known that with all the politicians the bull was rampant here in the state capitol, but I just did not know you could smell it so easily."

Daddy Would Have Loved It

Many of us have suffered through the awkwardness of inquiring about someone who has passed away. It can be an embarrassing situation, but it's just one of those things. I am often the recipient of those questions when I speak in Alabama. Both my parents were from Alabama and went to Auburn University. We ALL did. When I began my speaking career, I spoke often in that state, and people always came up when I finished speaking and asked if I were Cora and Jim Swanner's daughter. They had known a lot of people at Auburn, which was much smaller in the late thirties. Mother and Daddy passed away when they were in the prime of their lives (ages 53 and 55), and the questions that I had previously enjoyed answering after bookings became a little awkward . . . but very predictable.

Actually, it never failed after a speech in Alabama. Someone would come up and start the predictable questions.

"Say, was your maiden name Swanner?"

"Yes, it was."

"I was a fraternity brother of your father's at Auburn. How is Jim?"

"Well, I'm sorry to say, he passed away several years ago."

The inquirer's face falls. "I'm sorry," he says. There is an awkward silence. Then the person says, "I remember he married Cora Lipscomb. How is Cora doing?"

"Not well," I think to myself, but answer, "I'm sorry, but she passed away, too."

This exchange is so painful for some people that I must admit from time to time, I tried to avoid it by changing my answers. It did not work. When someone asked how Mother and Daddy were doing, I just answered, "Fine," but that usually led to a question like, "Do they ever get down to a football game?"

Even if I smiled to myself and said out loud, "They never miss a game," the individual would want to "get with 'em" at Homecoming. Once I said, "If they don't actually get to the game, they're there in spirit," but my sister Katherine said that was sick, and she knows about things like that because she's OLDER.

Sometimes you just have to be blunt, and that tactic will usually work well for all concerned if you remember to smile. We were at a dance in Burlington several years after Mother and Daddy died, and an older gentleman whom I did not know asked me to dance. As we moved along the floor, he said, "I've known your father and mother for years." I was startled and did not respond. Before I could think of anything to say, he continued,

"As a matter of fact, I saw your father last week and I don't believe he had ever looked better."

You just have to see the humor in a situation like this. I smiled and whispered, "The next time you see him, RUN LIKE HELL! He's been dead for years!"

Sometimes blunt humor—if said with a smile—is the best way to handle an awkward situation. And the Daddy who influenced me to have a sense of humor . . . would have loved it!

An Interesting Signal

During the transition from being Miss North Carolina to a full-time professional speaker, I emceed numerous beauty pageants throughout the South. It was great training because I never knew when a zipper would break or a prop would be misplaced, and I would have to keep the audience laughing while frantic activity went on backstage. It was also excellent training for seeing the humor in a variety of situations.

A recurring challenge at pageants was to develop a signal to let me know to fill the time until each contestant was ready to perform her talent. After trying all kinds of signaling methods, from red and green lights on the lectern to earphones hidden in my hair, I realized that the simplest method was for someone to tap me on the back from behind the curtain.

I stood at a lectern right in front of the curtain and when someone tapped my shoulder, the movement of the curtain was so slight that audiences never saw a thing. After the tap, I wrapped up my story and introduced the next contestant. It worked like a charm every time . . . except once.

The Jaycees of a very small town were putting on the pageant. The curtain man was appointed to signal me throughout the evening. He was a short fellow, very nice, and we had no problems with the tapping during the rehearsal. The pageant was a different story. While the stagehands set up for the first of the ten "talent" competitors, I launched into one of my little fillers as planned. The tap came . . . but not on my back. It was much lower.

It was a surprise, but I figured the guy just did not realize how much shorter he was than I. I introduced the first contestant and stepped back stage.

"That worked fine," I said, "but tap a little higher. On the shoulder." He nodded.

The next tap came in the exact same place. "Hum," I thought. "He must not be very smart." After I introduced the second contestant, I ducked behind the curtain again.

"Look," I whispered, staring right down into his eyes. "You're tapping me in the wrong place. You are missing my back and hitting my backside. There IS a difference. Get the tap up." He didn't say a word, but nodded again.

The third tap was the same as the first two, and at the end of the fourth tap I felt just a little rub. I quickly introduced the next talent contestant and headed backstage.

"Okay, buddy. You're through tapping. You got that? Don't tap me again. I'll just stand out front and GUESS when y'all have set up for the next contestant."

He finally spoke in a backstage whisper. "Do you mean that? No more tapping?"

"You're darn right I mean it. Keep your hands on the ropes."

With that he broke into a big grin. "Jeanne, I've gotta tell you something. A bunch of us decided to have a little lottery on the side. There are ten girls, so we put ten numbers in a hat and each drew one out. Then we put up ten bucks each to make a hundred dollar pot. I was to tap you in the wrong place and see how long you would put up with it. Whoever had the number on which you told me to stop tapping would win the pot. If you didn't ever say stop, number ten got all the money."

I stood there in disbelief, then whispered back, "That's one of the worst things I've ever heard!"

"Naw," he grinned. "The worst thing is that you told me to stop after tap number four . . . and I had number seven." He looked around to see if anyone else was listening. "Say, how about letting me tap you a few more times, and I'll split the hundred dollar pot with you."

I've always believed in seeing the humor in what could be an unpleasant situation. I don't remember exactly what I bought with that fifty dollars . . . .

A Split Decision

Jerry usually goes with me to nearby speaking engagements when it is necessary to drive rather than fly. On one such occasion, I was to speak at a banquet in a huge ballroom on the campus of one of our universities in North Carolina. I will not say which one . . . but it was in Raleigh. The agenda was fairly routine. First there was a banquet, then I was to speak, and then there would be a dance. I had spoken. I had done my part and was standing around with everyone else while people took down some of the tables and set up for the band . . . and I was smiling. Once you've been in the Miss America Pageant, you NEVER forget how to smiiile. Over the course of time, I must admit my beauty pageant smile has also become my "marriage smile." Women will understand what I am referring to. Every woman knows how she can stand around at something like a big cocktail party and have a broad smile on her face, and everyone will think she is the happiest person they have ever seen. And she can talk to her husband and never break that smile, and he will know . . . she is NOT HAPPY AT ALL.

That is the kind of smile I had on my face as I stood around after this particular banquet presentation. All of a sudden, my 6'6" husband hurried up to me and said, "Get your things. We're leaving." My smile never flinched as I talked to him through my teeth. "What do you mean 'we're leaving'? I told these people we would stay for the dance."

He whispered, "I DON'T CARE what you told anybody. We're going right now. I've RIPPED MY PANTS right down the back."

The man had a problem. Not only had he ripped his pants, but he must have been seated when it happened because they were standing wide open. But I had a problem too. I had told these people, "I would just LOVE to stay for the dance."

I had on a gorgeous, orange evening gown made out of three bolts of our North Carolina textiles. In my purse I had a spool of matching orange thread and a needle. I wish you could have seen his expression when I told him all we had to do was go somewhere and let him take off his pants for me to sew them up with orange thread. It took a few minutes, but I finally got him to realize this was what we had to do.

The only places this group had rented were the huge ball-room and the rest rooms. There was NO WAY I could sneak my body unnoticed into the men's rest room. Then I thought about the ladies rest room, and I thought about those little stalls. I said to myself, "If I can get him in there, and get him into one of those little stalls, I'm home free." Let's be candid. How many women would be in the ladies rest room between the banquet and the dance? EVERY woman there seemed lined up to get into that rest room.

I had spoken in that ballroom on many occasions, and I knew that down a dead-end hall, away from the main door, there was another ladies rest room that most people did not know about because they did not walk by it.

Jerry backed down the hall with me, sneaked into the ladies rest room, and took off his pants. You can probably get the pic-ture: A middle-aged man, nervously looking around, standing in the ladies rest room in his underwear. Question: Why do men start yelling at their wives at a time like this? I am a former coach who has never sewn much. I do well to thread a needle in good light in a room by myself, and here he was hopping from one foot to the other, telling me to "hurry up."

It was at that exact moment that we heard the female voices coming down the hall. It was evident where they were coming. We were at a dead end.

Jerry started frantically running around the room. You have never seen a six-foot-six man move as FAST in your life . . . but he was not going anywhere. I said, "Get in the stall!" He jumped in the stall, and I looked down and all I saw were two size twelve shoes. I shouted, "PUT YOUR FEET UP, OR GET OUT OF THE STALL!" He put his feet up, and his knees went up over the top of the stall door.

I said, "GET OUT OF THE STALL! They'll be here in a minute." He bolted out of the stall, and I screamed, "GET IN THE CLOSET!" He jumped into the closet, and I wadded up his pants and hid them behind my back just as two of the nicest ladies anyone would ever want to meet walked in.

They had been in the room about ten seconds when we heard this banging on the door, and Jerry's evidently male voice whispered in a panic, "Jeanne, OPEN the door." I wish you could have seen the two ladies when they heard a man's voice. I just stood there and acted as though I had not heard a thing. But then it got louder. "JEANNE, OP-EN-THE-DOOR!" He had never been afraid in the dark before, and I could not figure out what his problem was.

Then I heard in the loudest voice I have ever heard in my life . . . "JEANNE! PLEASE, OPEN THE DOOR! I'M OUT IN THE BALLROOM!"

Baton!

Do you remember when you were in a high school play, and it was your turn to say a line . . . and the line was gone?! Your mother

and daddy fell out into the aisle. THEY KNEW ALL THE
LINES. (My mother used to come in an identical costume . . .
just in case. You do not know when you'll get your "big break.")
And right before you literally passed out in front of your home
town, a prompter—with the book, of course—standing on a
stepladder behind the curtain, whispered a cue and you were
O.K.? The word "BATON" can be your cue . . . to see the humor in stressful, awkward, or unpleasant situations.

I was in a little bitty town in eastern North Carolina to
emcee the annual beauty pageant. The night of the rehearsal, I
asked one of the contestants, "What do you do for your talent?"
She smiled and said, "I twirl the baton."

I must be honest. All I could think of was, "Oh no. Not
another baton twirler." I can not even remember how many
baton twirlers I have seen after years of emceeing pageants.

I do not know much about twirling the baton, having spent
all of my spare time growing up playing basketball and perfect-
ing my hook shots. We begged for me to shoot hook shots for my
talent in the Miss America Pageant but the pageant officials
said, "No. No. No." Sometimes I wonder if they were afraid I
might win. The headlines would have read: "HOOKER WINS
MISS AMERICA!"

However, there are a couple of things I know about twirling
the baton. For one thing, it is more difficult than most people
think. The baton does not just fall in your hand and start
twirling itself around and pulling your arm through the air. It
goes in and out of your fingers some way. Secondly, twirling the
baton is just like many things in this world: if you want to be
good, really good—and I have seen some people who are—you
have to practice for years. Yearrrrrrrrrrrs. Unfortunately, this
contestant only had . . . two weeks.

She decided to be in the pageant at a late date, and almost
changed her mind when the officials reminded her, "You've got
to have three minutes worth of talent." But she thought about it,

and decided that since her younger sister in the second grade had a baton, she would borrow the thing . . . and twirl for her talent. The music she had selected was "The Hustle."

The night of the rehearsal she got out in the center of the stage, and she did not twirl the baton AT ALL! She held it smack dab in the middle and twisted her wrist back and forth, back and forth, back and forth as faaaaast as she could move her arm, trying to make it appear from a distance—in a dark auditorium—that she was twirling the baton.

When I saw what she was doing, I stepped back stage to one of the Jaycees and said, "I have got to talk to somebody. She's NOT twirling the baton!"

He said, "Well, WE KNOW THAT." Then he added, looking out at the contestant in the center of the stage, "But isn't she purtty?"

I swallowed hard and said, "You don't seem to understand the world situation as it is today. Being pretty is not an important thing. Right now, the main thing is . . . she's going to make a fool out of herself tomorrow night in front of her hometown!"

I will never forget his response. He looked up at me and said, "Naw, I think you're the one who doesn't understand, Jeanne. You just breezed in here tonight as the out-of-town expert. We've been working with this girl for two weeks. She's got more personality than all the other contestants in the pageant put together. She just doesn't have any talent! Leave her alone and let her do what she can do."

Then he said something about her that I very much want people to say about me after every speaking engagement. He said something I believe most of us would like for people to say about us: "After working with her for two weeks, we've decided we want her to win. She's so pleasant, we know we would enjoy working with her for the coming year."

He did not say, "She'll win the state pageant." He did not say again, "She's so purtty." HE SAID, "She's so pleasant that we know we would enjoy working with her for the coming year." What a compliment!

This contestant had one tiny hope of gaining any points in the talent division. About a minute and fifteen seconds into her three-minute routine, she rared back, and got ready to TOSS that baton up into the air . . . once. She had no control over where it went. People who had been at rehearsal for two weeks knew: DUCK when she gets ready to throw the thing! They came in old football helmets; and when it was time for the toss, mothers would casually reach over, put their hands on the children's heads, and just push them down into their seats. Wherever the baton went, she went after it and would catch it with both hands . . . and for the rest of her allotted time she stood there twisting her wrist back and forth, back and forth.

You were not there. I was there. I cannot make stuff like this up. It actually happened in 1973, but everybody has "been there." As I describe the situation, think about it carefully. We have all been in settings and situations that were similar. We have all been there.

It was in the summer and it was hot. Had been almost a hundred degrees OUTSIDE that day. The pageant was in an old, wooden, elementary school auditorium with no air conditioning. Sticks were holding all of the windows open, which I thought was very interesting because . . . the windows were all broken out!

Eight hundred people were jammed inside and the place only seated six hundred and fifty. People were everywhere. A woman in the front row had one of those curved Popsicle-stick, cardboard, "funeral home fans" (with a picture of Heaven on the backside) and she was fanning her chest. She never missed a beat. I could barely emcee the pageant for watching her work that fan.

A slick salesman had come through town selling walkie-talkies, and every Jaycee had one on his hip. Jaycees stood backstage with walkie-talkies only four feet from each other saying, "Can you hear me? Can you hear me? . . . Let up on the button, Bubba!"

They rolled out a piano for one of the contestants who stood beside it and announced, "I'm going to play a medley of Gershwin tunes that I wrote."

Have you "been there?" Sure. We've all "been there."

I normally stand at a lectern, introduce the contestant, and then get off stage. This night, I would not have left the stage for anything. I had to see if the baton twirler could fool even a single person.

The music of "The Hustle" started: Dun,dun,dun, ta-dun, ta-dun, dun-ta; dun,dun,dun, ta-dun, ta-dun, dun-ta (back and forth, back and forth, back and forth, back and forth). Eight hundred people sat in TOTAL DISBELIEF. They almost could not comprehend what they were seeing. I knew they were in shock because they all leaned forward in their seats at the same time, and out of the corner of my eye, I saw the woman slow-ly put down the funeral home fan.

But did they burst out laughing? Noooo. They did not know WHAT they were supposed to do. They did not know whether she was trying to do comedy, or what. It was as though eight hundred people leaned forward even further and whispered, "GIVE US A CUE. WHAT DO YOU WANT US TO DO?"

I maintain that in every situation when there is more than one person involved and something happens that is a little unpleasant, stressful, awkward or embarrassing, people stand around and wait on a cue. If the cue is to get angry, most people will get angry. If the cue is to fall apart, people fall apart; but if the cue is to see the humor in the situation, they will pick it up and run with it, and be more effective. If only one person is involved, it is up to that person to cue himself to keep a sense of humor.

For one minute and fifteen seconds she stood in the center of the stage with the baton in her hand, twisting it back and forth, back and forth, and the people in the audience held back the laughter. It was not easy. Judges broke their pencils. Mothers slid their hands over their children's mouths. But they had mentally told themselves they could hold back anything for just three minutes. But they did not know about the BIG TOSS.

At a minute and fifteen seconds, the "twirler" rared back. Jaycees got on their knees and started praying, "Let her catch it, please. Don't let her knock somebody out." And in front of her hometown of eight hundred people, she tossed that baton up into the air . . . and it did not come back down. I repeat: IT JUST DID NOT COME BACK DOWN!

Now, the music did not know it had not come back down. The music kept right on going, "dun,dun,dun, ta-dun, ta-dun, dun-ta." I am sure you can see the picture. Here was this young woman—panic-stricken—looking all around on stage for the baton. She looked over at me and I mouthed, "I don't have it." She looked out at the audience, and it was as though all those people, at the same time, shrugged and said, "We don't either." The baton was lodged up in the curtains . . . and it was not coming down!

Participation in pageants is often viewed as unimportant. But if you are eighteen-years old and have made the decision to be in one, and if you are on stage twirling a baton in front of your hometown AND YOU DO NOT HAVE A BATON, you tell me what could be more important? Remember, it was a tiny town. The kind of town where, when she was eighty-years-old she could go in the grocery store and someone would say, "Do you remember that night she was twirling that baton?"

If that had been me, I would either have fainted or I would have pretended to faint. Eighteen people would have had to drag my body right off that stage. However, at age eighteen, she had what I have been talking about this entire book. SHE HAD A SENSE OF HUMOR.

Incidentally, she had the same choices we have every day. She could have stomped off that stage and just before she disappeared behind the curtain, turned to the audience and in an angry voice, said, "Those Jaycees!" People pick up on cues so quickly that half of the audience would have immediately assumed the Jaycees had done something. They had not done a thing. They did not have a man up in the curtains who reached out and grabbed the baton as it went by.

She could have burst into tears and run off the stage. Remember, she was only eighteen. Everyone would have shaken their head and said, "What a shame, what a shame." They would have had that sick feeling you get in your stomach when you know somebody did not handle a situation the best way possible.

But she decided to see the humor in it. When she did, I stood on the side of the stage and watched her literally influence eight hundred people to see the humorous side of the situation with her.

She looked up, and she saw that the baton was in the curtains and it was not coming down. She jumped up and down on the stage a couple of times . . . trying to jar the auditorium. But the baton was NOT coming down.

She looked out and saw eight hundred people who were by that point about to explode, but doing their best to hold in their laughter. She heard the music, knew she had about a minute left, and she made a snap decision to see the humor in the situation and make the most of it.

She gave all of those people her best beauty pageant smile . . . and . . . she started pantomiming a baton routine, THE LIKES OF WHICH, YOU HAVE NEVER SEEN. She pretended to toss that baton UP, and faked catching it behind her neck. She pretended to twirl it around her waist. People went crazy!

She danced to the left side of the stage and then to the right, all the time moving her wrist with an exaggerated twirling motion.

She pretended to toss the baton up a second time . . . and

mimicked watching it take loops in the air. I looked out, and eight hundred heads were rolling around, watching it take loops with her. Just before it hit the stage, she reached under her leg and pretended to catch it.

By now mothers were throwing their babies up into the air! But did she let well enough alone? Not this girl. You never quit when you are on a roll, and she had 'em in the palm of her hand. She danced to the side of the stage, and pretended to catch a SECOND BATON. And when the music ended, she was standing in the center of the stage pretending to twirl two batons as fast as she could.

. . . A man in the back row said to his wife, "SHE'S TWIRLING THEM SO FAST, I CAN'T EVEN SEE THE BATONS!!!!"

It's Your Turn to Work Magic

As a reminder to see the humor in stressful, awkward, or potentially unpleasant situations, you may want to write down the word "Baton." Put it on an index card. You may even want to write it on ten index cards and sprinkle them around your house or business. The next time something happens, and you do not believe you will be able to see the humor in it, pull out that card and read the one word. It will serve as a reminder that if an eighteen-year-old young woman could see the humor while standing on stage in front of her hometown people for the purpose of twirling a baton . . . AND SHE DOESN'T HAVE A BATON . . . then we can see the humor in any stressful, awkward, or unpleasant situations that occur in our lives.

I repeat. Write it down. The word is . . . BATON.

Potion 7
Take Humor Breaks/
Collect Humor Cues

A fter graduating from Auburn University, I taught physical education and coached for nine years while continuing to speak on weekends and during the summer. Some people may wonder "coached what?" but all women physical educators from that era know the answer to that is . . . coached everything. However, my emphasis was on basketball. During those teaching and coaching years, I never ceased to be amazed at the phenomenon of the teachers' lounge break.

When there was a break in the schedule, teachers dropped by the school lounge to grab a cup of coffee, eat a snack, or just chat with a friend. In theory, "taking a little break" sent them back to the classroom rejuvenated and ready for the next students. We also see this practice in most business situations:

folks gathered at the coffee pot or in the company's kitchen taking a break.

I am certainly not opposed to gathering places in any work environment, or socializing, but I do suggest if an individual is in a pressure or stressful situation, or is just tired, a break at the favorite gathering place may not be what the doctor ordered. In fact, it may do more harm than good. Gathering places are often where rumors fly, rumors that may upset people when they hear them. A person needing a little break does not need to spend the time listening to another's problems or learning there may be unexpected work on the way. When this happens, people usually leave their breaks more upset or bothered than they were ten minutes earlier. Some break!

An exercise break has often been suggested as a way to relieve stress and become rejuvenated. Although I cannot deny that exercise breaks will provide you with physical and mental benefits, I would suggest that a humor break is an alternative which will offer some of the same benefits. I recommend taking a humor break at least once a day.

TAKING HUMOR BREAKS

Taking a "Humor Break" is using a few minutes during the day to sit back, relax, refer to your humor cues, and just laugh. It is taking a break not only from what you are doing, but also from the surroundings and the people with whom you are working. A humor break puts you into a world of your own for just a few minutes, and lets you forget work and everything associated with it.

People generally agree that if something happens during the workday that is funny, and they laugh for a few minutes, they feel relaxed. For those few seconds, they forget the pressures at hand. That is why after my speeches, one of the greatest compliments I receive is, "You made me forget my problems for a little while." Someone said, "Humor is a lot like changing a baby's diaper. It does not offer a permanent solution, but it makes things much more tolerable for a little while." Humor is a morale booster at work and at home. We like to laugh. It makes us feel good. It is like a slap. Thanks, I needed that.

But we do not always work around people who are funny, and if we do, we cannot count on them for humor every time we need a little shot in the arm. No, it is better to have a special time set aside for a humor break and an organized way to insure that break is successful.

COLLECTING HUMOR CUES

Several years ago, I started collecting a set of what I call "Humor Cues": personal experiences, stories, jokes, etc. that work magic on Jeanne Robertson. They make me laugh. Whenever I take a humor break, I pull out something from my collection and let it cue my funny bone to go to work. For just a few minutes, I am in my own little world, far away from the problems of the day. The situation is reminiscent of "Everybody's Got a Laughin' Place" from Uncle Remus. My laughin' place is wherever I want it to be . . . and whenever I want it to be. The break may last only a couple of minutes. It is a tremendous device that not only serves as a truly refreshing break, but also influences me to continue to develop my sense of humor. Everything in my humor cue collection is guaranteed to make me laugh. My particular cues might not tickle anyone else's funny bone, just as the ones you collect may work only on you. That is why complete joke books cannot serve as a person's humor cue collection. You may read through five pages of jokes before finding one that really makes you laugh. The cues you collect should be guaranteed to make YOU laugh immediately.

When I take a humor break, I turn to my cues and pull out just one. If it is something that needs to be read, I read it. If it is one word to remind me of an hilarious event, I sit back and think about the event. The results are the same. In just a few seconds, I am smiling and far away from the pressures of the day.

I am very picky about what goes into my cue collection. When I am tired, something that brings a slight smile to my face is not adequate. I need a laugh. So I gather my humor cues very carefully both from my personal experiences and other sources.

ORGANIZING HUMOR CUES

I have tried several ways of organizing my cues, and have found the best way is simply to drop them into files. When I take a break, I pull out whatever is in front of the current file, enjoy it, and store it at the back of the file. This means the cues do not roll around often, which makes them just that much funnier. As your personal humor collection grows, you will notice that they roll around so seldom, you have usually forgotten them.

Begin your humor collection by reminiscing about humorous personal experiences, and then jot down a few key words— separate sheets of paper for each event—that will serve as reminders. As a humorist, most of the personal experiences which I have included in my humor file are written in story form, but I do not recommend this technique for most people. I write up my funny experiences only to perfect the wording used in speeches. Otherwise, only a few key words would be sufficient. In some instances, the humorous experiences cannot be described in words. Often an experience is an "HTBT," a "Had To Be There." No amount of writing or telling will capture the hilarity of the happening. For example, I could report in detail a story involving my husband and an elderly man standing in the second pew at our church. It would not matter how meticuously and vividly I describe the event, there is no way it will bring laughter to anyone but my husband and me. It's an "HTBT." You had to be there. All we need are the words, "elderly man, standing, Front Street Church" and my husband and I both burst out laughing. So begin your humor collection by making a list of key words that help you recall the situation and make you laugh.

Initially, your recall of funny experiences may not offer a long list of humor cues. But surely the thoughts about your childhood, college days, bringing up children, or your work experiences will provide you with a dozen or so experiences that make you burst out laughing. Add to your humor file the best old jokes, stories, or anecdotes that you can recall. If your humor file is still not large, do not worry. For your humor break to be successful, you do need a large number of items. But if humor becomes a significant part of your lifestyle, this will not be a problem. Your humor cue collection will grow rapidly. As your collection grows and as you change over the years, your challenge will then be to continue to refine the contents of your collection.

As you begin to collect personal humor cues, it is important to remember that you are the only person a piece of material is intended to make laugh. It is your cue to make you laugh during your humor break.

MY HUMOR CUES

Throughout this book I have shared excerpts from my personal humor cue collection which have often magically made my day. As you have already surmised, most of the humor that tickles my funny bone comes from my personal experiences. If these stories or the next few experiences do not make you laugh, or even make you smile, it will be a perfect illustration of my point that stories strike people in different ways. Or, maybe Genie better stay in her bottle. Read on as I share a few more personal stories from my collection. They serve my purpose during my humor breaks. Perhaps they will also serve yours! More importantly, perhaps you will begin your own humor cue collection full of reminders that make you laugh.

NCAA Finals

I never speak in New Orleans that I am not reminded of speaking there on Tuesday morning, March 30, 1982. The date means nothing . . . unless you are an avid basketball fan, as I am, or unless you are a fan of either the University of North Carolina or Georgetown University basketball teams. My speech on that date was given the morning AFTER the finals of the NCAA tournament when those two teams met for the championship.

Fans do not know whether their team will be in the Final Four until the week before the games. When it became apparent the Tarheels would be making the trip, everybody was trying to get transportation from North Carolina to Louisiana. Plane tickets were scarce, as were hotel rooms and tickets to the game.

I had a plane ticket because this speech had been booked for months, and I had a room reservation at the location of the convention. I did not, however, have a ticket to the game.

All of my friends wanted to know, "Can you get a ticket to the game?" "Are you going to the game?"

I was straightforward and told them like it was. "You know I've got a plane ticket and a hotel room," I said. "I do not at this point have a ticket for the game. But you know me well, so you know that when I get to New Orleans, I WILL GET a ticket to the game."

Take it from one who has been there. You do not know what awkward is until you stand on the streets of New Orleans . . . a woman, by yourself . . . shouting, "NAME YOUR PRICE!"

Mrs. Bowden

I guess we all had at least one high school teacher like Mrs. Bowden, a teacher who had developed the habit of slipping her hand in her blouse several times during every class and pulling up a mysterious strap. To be fair, at times she DID try to be discreet, usually waiting to "pull up" until the students were involved in class assignments or until she was walking toward the storage cabinet in the back of the room. However, it was such a habit with her that she was just as likely to reach right for her shoulder when a student was standing at her desk.

Mrs. Bowden's bad habit would have been long forgotten by maturing students if it had not been for that one day she "did the class in." Working at the blackboard, she turned to face the students at EXACTLY the same time she reached in her blouse and said, "Class, I have something to show you."

The class was NEVER quite the same again.

A Special Invitation

Here are the closing lines of a letter received in my office:

"We certainly hope Jeanne Robertson will be available to speak at our banquet. Unfortunately we are short of funds, but there are a number of influential people in our club, and I can't help but think she will obtain many bookings on the spot if she will just expose herself to them."

Team Motivation

During a trip to Detroit, I had lunch with a fellow member of the National Speakers Association who was a motivational speaker. I had never heard him speak and did not know exactly what he spoke about, but something he related was of great interest to me.

It seems that for three years he had occasionally given motivational speeches to the Detroit Lions before games. I knew that the Lions were not exactly dominating the NFL at that time, so I kept my mouth shut at first. He went on to say that he did the same thing for Michigan State on a more regular basis.

Now THAT I found very interesting. I wanted to know what one would say to a football team week after week. He admitted it was a difficult task and added that he had an especially tough job the following weekend. That next Saturday, he was to motivate the Michigan State team (2-7) right before they played Ohio State (7-2).

Tough? I would call it almost impossible. I could not believe a speaker would put himself in that position. I asked, "Don't you hesitate to take money for something you might not be able to produce? What if they don't win?"

He shook his head and leaned forward as though he was telling me a secret. "If I weren't there, they might not go down on the field."

A Burned Slip

I live in a rush and I like it. Would not have it any other way. In one of my typical "running late, get packed, get to the airport" mornings, I was ironing a half slip. The phone rang, the iron got too hot while I was talking, and I burned an iron-size hole in the slip the second I returned to my task. You get the picture. I mumbled a few words like "my goodness," threw the slip in the trash can, and started rummaging through the drawers trying to find another one. Everything was the wrong length, so I decided to just finish packing and stop on my way out of town and buy a new one.

Twenty minutes later I stopped at a local department store and literally ran up to a little lady in the lingerie section and said, "Give me your longest half slip as fast as you can." I think I scared her because she jumped a little. But she hurried to a table, picked up a half slip that would go from her shoulders to her knees, and said, "This is it. Eight dollars."

I held it to my waist and it looked right, so I said, "I'll take it," and shoved a twenty dollar bill into her hand.

She took the slip from me and headed toward the register saying, "I'll put it in a bag."

"That's not necessary," I said hurriedly. "I don't need a bag. I don't have on a slip. While you make change, I'll just step behind a rack and put it on." She looked at me a little funny, but did not say anything.

As I came out from behind the rack, I noticed a long table piled high with underpants for $1.50 per pair. I remember thinking, "Darn, I need some underwear, but I don't have time to shop." Then, noticing the price again, I grabbed one pair in my size and headed for the register. "Wait a minute," I said quickly to the lady. "Take one pair of underpants out of my change."

The clerk thought for a few seconds as she gazed at the money in her hand. She never lifted her head when she slowly drawled, "Are you gonna be needing a bag?"

What Next?

My Uncle Mac and Aunt Libba ran away and got married. They were going to keep it a secret and go ahead and have a big wedding at some later date, but they began to feel bad about doing that and decided to tell. They knew that they had better break the news gently to their parents and decided to do so in stages.

Several days after making this decision, they were eating lunch with my grandparents, Papa and Grandma Freddie. Sometime between "this looks good" and "I can't eat another bite" the newlyweds said they had something to tell them, and proceeded to announce they were engaged.

The older couple was thrilled and immediately began calling everyone in the family to share the news. Seeing how excited everyone was that afternoon when they heard about the upcoming wedding, Mac and Libba started feeling worse and decided to go ahead and tell the truth.

At dinner that same night, the young couple said they again had something to tell Papa and Grandma Freddie. They went on to say that they had run away and were already married.

Papa slowly put down his fork and looked at them in silence for a few seconds before finally saying, "God, I'm afraid to come down for breakfast."

Unexpected Voices

I had heard someone had invented a device for your refrigerator that said things like "Are you sure you want something to eat?" when you opened the door. And I knew certain new makes of automobiles had recorded messages such as, "You are low on gas." But I had never seen, or heard of, a talking soft drink machine. The world should be warned about such inventions.

When staying during a speaking trip at The Abbey, a resort located on Lake Geneva in Wisconsin, I went into the hallway to find the soft drink machine that the hotel operator promised was located somewhere in the vicinity of my room. (Two points here: (1) The words "in the vicinity of your room" mean different things to different people, and (2) While I was on the phone, she COULD HAVE MENTIONED the machine was alive.) It was very late at night and the halls were deserted, but I finally wound my way around to the desolate area where the vending machine was located. The drinks were seventy-five cents, but I had come so far and had so much time invested by that point, I decided to be a big spender. I shoved the two quarters I had in my hand through the slot before rummaging through my purse for the rest of the money. In a few seconds, a voice boomed slowly and deliberately, "YOU-DID-NOT-PUT-IN-ENOUGH-MONEY!"

Because I knew there were no other people in sight AND since I evidently missed the announcement that soft drink machines had learned to talk and would be scaring us in the middle of the night in desolate areas of hotels, my body jolted in such a way that I cut five years off of my life span.

I am not the panicky or frightful type, and did not question whether or not I was hearing things. I KNEW I had heard what I heard. The question was: Who said it?

I slowly turned my head from side to side to see if someone were hiding behind a door or post. I did not see anyone so I cautiously asked, "Who's there?" Silence. I could not help but think, "People are getting beaten up and robbed all over this country

because they are in places they have no business being, drinking
and carrying on. Here I am in a respectable hotel . . . several
floors away from the bar and all the partying . . . just trying to
get a diet drink . . . and somebody's gonna rob me right here and
now." "I KNOW you're there," I managed to blurt out.

The machine did not say a word. By then I was scared, but
not so scared that I would leave fifty cents in the machine. So I hit
the coin return to get my money and get out of there. I must have
hit it wrong because the quarters did not come out, but the voice
spoke again, "YOU-DID-NOT-PUT-IN-ENOUGH-MONEY!"

A sense of relief spread through my body because this time I
knew "who" . . . or should I say "what" was talking to me. I do
not like most machines, and I certainly do not like ones that
correct me or give orders. Therefore, I am at a loss to explain why
I stood there for a few seconds and then leaned forward and asked
the machine, "HOW-MUCH-MORE-DO-YOU-WANT?"

Audience Feedback

At one point in my career, I competed in the Great Atlanta Laff
Off for Showtime Cablevision. Five of us were featured in the
televised competition that was held before a live audience of
1300 people. My family and a few close friends gathered in
Atlanta to cheer me on. When I had finished my allotted fifteen minutes, they quickly gathered around to tell me they were
SURE I would win. Of course, they told me that before I even
walked on the stage.

I finished fourth out of the five. As loyal friends and family
have a tendency to do, they again gathered around after the announcements to tell me that I "SHOULD have won." Our son was
more honest.

We noticed Beaver was not anywhere to be seen at the conclusion of the taping, and it turned out he was so upset when I came in
fourth that he had walked back to the hotel. When we returned to

the room, he opened the door and with tears in his eyes, shouted, "Mom, you were ROBBED! You should have come in SECOND!"

Instant Recognition

One summer I was to speak at an international convention of an organization of high school students. The day before I was to fly to New Orleans for the meeting, my telephone rang and an apprehensive young voice asked, "Is this Jeanne Robertson?"

"Yes."

"The Jeanne Robertson who gives speeches?"

"Yes." (It's always best to admit it.)

I could sense the young man's relief as he let out a sigh. "OH, THANK GOODNESS," he said. "I've been calling all over the state of North Carolina looking for you." (note: There isn't a parent of a teenager anywhere who does not know to WHOM those long distance calls were charged.)

The caller identified himself and said, "I'm the person who will meet you at the airport tomorrow and take you to your hotel."

I sensed an urgency in his voice and was perplexed. This was a fairly routine procedure. "Fine, I look forward to meeting you in person."

"NOOOO," he responded. "It is NOT fine. My high school adviser gave me a little piece of paper that had your time of arrival and flight number written on it and he said, 'Whatever you do, DON'T LOSE this piece of paper,' . . . and I'VE LOST IT!"

No one should ever forget what it was like when a high school adviser said TO DO or NOT TO DO something. "There's no problem," I assured him, and got my ticket to give him the information.

We chatted a few minutes about the number of people who would be at the convention, who else was on the program, etc., and we were ready to hang up when he said, "There's one more thing. How will I recognize you?"

I smiled to myself. "Son, barefooted, with my hair MASHED DOWN, I am six feet, two inches tall. I will be wearing shoes . . . I ALWAYS wear shoes when I leave North Carolina . . . and that will make me about six-foot four. Also, I will be carrying a small, black ukulele case."

He paused for a couple of seconds and asked, "Do you know yet what you'll be wearing?"

The Royal Flush

One of the most difficult parts of assuming the parental or managerial role is knowing when to step back and let people do things on their own. It is often easier to take over and make sure something is handled the way we would want it handled than to let others venture forth and perhaps make mistakes. Every time I find it difficult to step back, I remind myself of something that happened in my family a few years ago.

By the time my granddaddy reached his nineties, my grandmother assumed the role of handling everything for him. It was true that he did need assistance with a number of tasks and she was younger, but she insisted on taking over everything. Many times he would politely say, "Susie, I can do this for myself," but she would ignore him and take charge. If he sat down to eat, she would begin to cut up his food. If he walked slowly toward the mailbox, she would hurry ahead and bring the mail back to him. Sometimes he would shake his head at me, and I knew he was thinking what he had expressed so often, "I can do this by myself." He was a gentle man, though, and other than comments such as these, he rarely ever complained. Everything she did was out of love, and down deep he knew it. But even love has its limits.

I was having Thanksgiving dinner with them down in Luverne, Alabama, and the routine was as I described. He wanted a big helping of beans; she gave him a small portion. I heard him mutter, "I wanted a few more than that." He began to salt his food, and she took the shaker from him and proceeded. He muttered, "I can do that by myself." You get the picture.

About halfway through the dinner, the old gentleman stood up, and reached for his cane, saying, "I think I'm sick." Leaving the dining room, he moved up the hall toward the bathroom as fast as he could.

Grandbubba—as we called her—jumped up to help him, but he mumbled over his shoulder "I can be sick by myself." I made her sit back down, and we both sat there for a few long minutes. Finally, she just could not stand it any longer, and said, "I need to help him," and hurried to the bathroom. I followed her. The door to the bathroom was closed, but we could hear him inside. He was sick and throwing up.

Grandbubba knocked on the door and asked if she could come in. He said, "No, I can handle this." She stood there a few minutes and tried again, "Cleveland, please let me help you." He managed to answer and again said, "Susie, I can DO THIS by myself."

She really did try, but she just could not step back and stop "taking over." After a few more seconds, she threw open the bathroom door to discover him sitting on a little chair next to the commode. Without giving him a chance to say a word, she surveyed the situation, rushed over and mashed down on the commode handle.

He sat there for a few moments, shoulders collapsed in frustration and then he slowly raised his head and said, "Thank you. Thank you. Thank you, Susie. You've just FLUSHED MY TEETH right down the toilet!"

Young Entrepreneur

My sister Andrea was seven years old when I won the title of Miss North Carolina. She was impressed. So impressed, in fact, that when I returned home from the pageant, she asked for my autograph. In a few days, she asked for another, then another. One does not have to be overly intelligent to figure out exactly what she was doing. She was selling them for twenty-five cents apiece to kids up and down the street. People in Graham thought that was cute. At nineteen, I was not so sure. I stopped giving her the autographs, and she began tearing the signatures off the bottom of old letters. In typical sibling style, I politely asked her to stop. "Sell another one of those signatures, Andrea, and I'll knock your nose to the back of your head!"

Several weeks later I was taking a bath, and like most people, I do not wear any clothes when I take a bath. About the time I was getting relaxed—as relaxed as a six-foot-two person can get in a tub—I heard the bathroom door squeak open, and several pairs of feet shuffle in. I peeped around the edge of the tub, and there was Andrea with two ten-year-old boys from up the street. When they saw me, Andrea pointed in my direction and said, "There she is . . . Miss North Carolina in the tub! One dollar, please!"

A Special Warning

I was in a small town to emcee a Miss North Carolina preliminary being held in an elementary school auditorium. The contestants and I were ushered into a third grade classroom which had been converted into a dressing room by taping construction paper over the windows and placing mirrors at the small school desks. Scattered around the room were children's handmade signs proclaiming "Welcome," "Smile," and "Good Luck!" It was evident that the teacher in this particular classroom had made the pageant a fun event for all the students. Each of the little people had left at their desks letters of encouragement for the contestants.

The following note was taped to the back of one chair: "Dear beuty girl. Do not fix up at this desk. It ant brung me nothin but bad luck."

The Best Ingredient

At a "Woman of the Year" banquet at a local YWCA in Arkansas, the ladies at the head table told me that we were having the specialty of the house for dessert. The recipe came from their new "Y" cookbook which they said was one of the best cookbooks around.

"Of course," one of the ladies whispered matter-of-factly, "we had to leave out a few of the dishes. In the last cookbook, some of the recipes called for whisky, and we were very criticized." Several ladies around me nodded in agreement.

A few seconds later, one of them leaned my way and mumbled, "Kept out some of the BEST recipes."

A Tall Order

The day before I left for a booking in Michigan, my contact called to double-check everything. "People up here are certainly looking forward to your coming," he said. "We've had good publicity about the SIX-FOOT-TWO lady speaker."

"Good," I said.

He continued. "One headline read 'TALLEST Miss America Contestant To Speak at Banquet.' Another read, 'Former TALL Basketball Player to be Chamber Guest!' I guess you could say everybody is looking forward to LOOKING UP to you."

"Great. I'm looking forward to speaking at the banquet."

"As a matter of fact," he added, "when you get here you really don't have to be so funny . . . but you DARN WELL BETTER BE TALL!"

If the Shoe Fits, Go for it!

I do not know what other women will pay for a good pair of shoes, but a woman who wears a size 11 will pay whatever is asked: $75?, $100?, $120? Sure, I'll pay that for good-looking shoes that fit my feet. My problem is FINDING good-looking shoes that fit my feet. With that in mind, you can imagine how excited I was to find a pair of stylish evening shoes in my size during a speaking trip.

It was one of those "we fit everybody" shoe stores that had boxes and boxes of shoes lining the walls. I headed for the end of the ladies' section and could not believe my eyes. Right there on the "Size 11 and Up" rack was a pair of stylish evening shoes. At first I thought they must have been put in the wrong place, but no, they fit.

I was so excited that I almost started hyperventilating. I grabbed the box and clutched it to my chest as I looked from side to side. It was as though I thought someone would jump out and rip the shoes out of my hands. Looking back on it, I guess I resembled a dog that had found a bone.

With my prized possession firmly in my grip, I hurried to the check-out counter and nervously shifted my weight back and forth from foot to foot as the clerk waited on other customers. Finally it was my turn. I put the box on the counter and leaned forward. "How much for these shoes?"

The clerk turned the box over a couple of times and answered nonchalantly, "Fourteen dollars."

I reeled at the thought. My mouth dried up. Gasping, it took me a few seconds before I could blurt out, "FOURTEEN DOLLARS!"

The lady looked around the room, then leaned over the counter in my direction. "Okay," she whispered in a low voice, "How 'bout twelve?"

The Clinging Cat

I was invited to attend a breakfast meeting the morning after a speaking engagement in Shreveport, Louisiana. It was for a group of business people who met once a month just to get to know each other better and swap business leads. One person was featured each month, and this month a young veterinarian told about his practice. Along with presenting statistical information, he explained that his work could be very interesting and told of something that had recently happened in his office.

Late one afternoon, a woman ve-ry, ve-ry slow-ly opened the door to his office and began to inch her way toward the receptionist's desk. Her clothes were disheveled, her hose torn, and there were scratches on her arms and legs. A cat was perched on her right shoulder, clinging for dear life. They were both walleyed and appeared equally scared to death. No one was with the woman, so she had apparently driven to the building with the cat in place, or vice versa.

The animal had literally dug into the lady's shoulder and neck. The woman and the cat were in frenzied states; hair was standing straight up on both of them. Ve-ry de-lib-er-ate-ly and without mov-ing her head, the woman mouthed to the receptionist, "I-NEED-to-see-the-vet." A classic understatement. The receptionist leaped from her chair and within seconds was following the doctor back into the lobby.

Still being careful not to move, the woman slowly mouthed to the doctor, "This-cat-has-been-sick-for-a-week."

"And you JUST brought it in?" the vet asked in bewilderment while reaching up to try to pry the animal loose. The cat hung on with the strength of a tiger, practically strangling the lady.

The woman looked at the doctor in disbelief, as she explained in choked terms, "I COULDN'T CATCH IT 'TIL TODAY."

GENERAL HUMOR

Reminiscing about your personal humorous experiences and those of your family, friends, and acquaintances should be the starting point for your humor file. Of course, my own humor file includes not only the anecdotes in this chapter, but also many of the amusing incidents in previous chapters. This portion of your humor file will probably not be large initially, but it will expand rapidly as humor becomes a conscious element of your lifestyle.

Although personal humor has been emphasized in this book, a humor file is not complete without "general" humor—humor that is available to the general public through oral or published sources. You may want to begin by reading several joke books and selecting only the jokes that make you burst out laughing. Then begin to clip newspaper reports, magazine articles, and cartoons that tickle your funny bone. Also, jot down any joke you hear that really gives you a laugh. Remember that your sole objective is to file things that make you laugh.

The following pages are a few examples of "general" humor that are included in my humor file. Some are very old stories or jokes, but when read occasionally, they still make me laugh. If you are affected the same way, you may want to include several of them—or any of my personal stories included in this book—in your humor file.

The Brick Story

Dear Sir:

I am writing in response to your request for additional information. In block #3 of the Accident Reporting Form I put "trying to do the job alone" as the cause of my accident. You said in your letter that I should explain more fully, and I trust that the following details will be sufficient.

I am a bricklayer by trade. On the day of the accident, I was working alone on the roof of a new six-story building. When I had completed my work, I discovered that I had about 500 pounds of bricks left over. Rather than carry the bricks down by hand, I decided to lower them in a barrel by using a pulley which fortunately was attached to the side of the building at the 6th floor.

Securing the rope at ground level, I went up to the roof, swung the barrel up, and loaded the bricks into it. Then I went back to the ground and untied the rope, holding it tightly to insure a slow descent of the 500 pounds of bricks. You will note in block number eleven of the Accident Reporting Form that I weigh 135 pounds.

Due to my surprise at being jerked off the ground so suddenly, I lost my presence of mind and forgot to let go of the rope. Needless to say, I proceeded at a rather rapid rate up the side of the building.

In the vicinity of the third floor, I met the barrel coming down. This explains the fractured skull and broken collarbone.

Slowed only slightly, I continued my rapid ascent, not stopping until the fingers of my right hand were two knuckles deep into the pulley. Fortunately, by this time I had regained my presence of mind and was able to hold tightly to the rope in spite of my pain.

At approximately the same time, however, the barrel of bricks hit the ground, and the bottom fell out of the barrel. Devoid of the weight of the bricks, the barrel now weighed approximately fifty pounds.

I refer you again to my weight in block number eleven. As you might imagine, I began a rapid descent down the side of the building. In the vicinity of the third floor, I met the barrel coming up. This accounts for the two fractured ankles and the lacerations of my legs and lower body. The encounter with the barrel slowed me enough to lessen my injuries. However, I fell onto the pile of bricks and fortunately only three vertebrae were cracked.

I am sorry to report, however, that as I lay on the bricks in pain, unable to stand and watching the empty barrel six stories above me, I again lost my presence of mind—and—I LET GO OF THE ROPE!!! The empty barrel weighed more than the rope, so it came back down on me and broke both of my legs.

I hope I have furnished the information you require as to how the accident occurred.

The House Visit

As the doctor made a house visit, the sick person's family gathered around, so the physician asked the private duty nurse to step into the bathroom with him to keep all the ears from hearing their discussion. They stepped into the small room and shut the door. Naturally, the family gathered around outside trying to hear.

Inside, the doctor put down the lid of the toilet and sat down while he and the nurse went over the patient's condition. When they finished their discussion, he stood to leave, and out of habit reached over and flushed the commode.

The family, eavesdropping outside the door, scattered . . . but continued to exchange quizzical looks as the doctor and nurse emerged from the bathroom.

Panting Dog

An executive in a large city advertising agency lived in an uptown apartment where he kept his two big dogs. His wife went away to visit relatives for a week, and he promised her he would leave his office twice a day at 11 A.M. and 4 P.M. and exercise the dogs. She claimed that if they didn't have their romp twice a day, they would get sick, so he said he'd do it.

Then he made a discovery. He found that whenever the telephone rang in the apartment, the two dogs would begin racing up and down the rooms and get plenty of exercise. All he had to do then was phone his apartment at eleven and again at four, let the bell ring fifteen times, then hang up. He told his associates about it to show them how smart he was.

One day, one of these associates managed to get the key to the apartment. He left the office quietly and went to the apartment just before four o'clock. He waited until the phone started ringing. He let it ring a dozen times, then lifted it off the hook, placed his face close to the mouthpiece, and began panting heavily—imitating a big dog. Then he hung up.

(H. Allen Smith, *The Compleat Practical Joker*)

I've Got a Secret

An elderly Senator was sitting beside a very beautiful blonde at a Washington party. During the course of the dinner, he put his hand under the table and started to feel her ankle. She gave him a sweet smile. Encouraged, he went a little further and reached the calf of her leg, and again the lady smiled. The Senator, thrilled by this encouragement, went about the knees. Suddenly, she smiled again, leaned in and whispered in his ear, "When you get far enough to discover that I'm a man, don't change the expression on your face. I'm Secret Agent Number Twelve!"

Communication Gaffe

A woman telephoned a friend. "How are you, dear?" she asked.

"Simply awful," came the reply. "My migraine headache has returned, my feet are killing me, my back is almost breaking in two, the ironing is piled to the ceiling, the house is a mess, and the children are driving me out of my mind."

"Now you listen to me," said the woman on the other end of the line. "You just go lie down and rest. I'll be right over and cook lunch for you and the children, get your ironing done, whisk up the house a bit, and watch the children while you get a bit of sleep. By the way, how is John?"

"John?" queried the complaining housewife.

"Yes, John," said the caller, "John, your husband."

"My husband's name isn't John."

"My gosh," gasped the caller, "I must have the wrong number."

There was a long stunned silence on the line until the woman finally said, "You're not going to come over, are you?"

Fading Memory

Among the passengers on one of her flights, an airline flight attendant told me, was a lady with a small boy and girl in tow. Shortly before lunch was to be served, the lady and her charges visited the toilets in the rear of the cabin. The lady sent the little boy into one of the rest rooms and accompanied the little girl into the other one.

The little boy finished his work, left the toilet, and headed back to his seat. An elderly man, who had been waiting, went into the cubicle the little boy had vacated.

In a moment or so, the woman and the little girl came out of the other toilet. The woman, thinking the little boy was still engaged, rapped sharply on the door across the aisle and said, "When you're finished, don't forget to zip your pants."

In a few moments, the elderly man emerged, stopped by the flight attendant and said, "Thanks, Miss. When you get old, you forget sometimes, and it's nice of the airline to have you girls remind us."

Fishy Tale

Two brothers fished together all the time. One of the brothers always caught fish while the other never did. One weekend they planned a big fishing trip, but at the last minute, the fish-catching brother became ill and stayed home. But he encouraged his brother, "Take my bait, my tackle and my boat and go catch some fish." Needless to say, the other brother was thrilled. He rose at the crack of dawn and went to the lake. "Boy," he said to himself, "I'm really going to catch the fish today!"

He fished with his brother's rod and reel, used his brother's bait, even sat in his brother's chair. Alas, after three hours he did not even have so much as one little nibble to show for his efforts. Then suddenly the waters of the lake parted, and a huge fish stuck up its head. "Where's your brother?" the fish asked.

Plain Facts

Perkins, generally considered the county derelict, was charged with shooting some pigeons that belonged to Spencer, a farmer.

Perkins' lawyer—a shrewd character named Vernon—tried to frighten the farmer.

"Now," said lawyer Vernon, "are you prepared to swear that this man shot your pigeons?"

"I didn't say he shot 'em," replied Spencer. "I said I suspected him of doing it."

"Ah! Now we're coming to it. What made you suspect Mr. Perkins?"

"First off, I caught him on my land with a gun. Second, I heard a gun go off and saw some pigeons fall. And third, I found four of my pigeons in Mr. Perkins' pocket, and I don't think the birds flew there and committed suicide."

Soul Mate

A woman and her grandmother—a very forgiving and religious soul—were sitting on their porch discussing a member of the family. "He's just no good," the young woman said. He's completely untrustworthy, not to mention lazy."

"Yes, he's bad, but Jesus loves him," the grandmother said as she rocked back and forth in her rocker.

"I'm not so sure of that," the younger woman persisted.

"Oh, yes," assured the elderly lady. "Jesus loves him." She rocked and thought for a few more minutes and then added, "Of course, Jesus doesn't know him like we do . . . ."

Accident Burden

A lady from the South was riding in a taxicab in New York when the driver slowed up a little to miss a pedestrian. Apparently, figuring that his unusual courtesy called for an explanation, he turned to the passenger to explain. "If you hit 'em," the cabby announced, "you gotta fill out a report."

False Conviction

One of three drinking buddies died and his body was down at the local funeral home. The day before he was supposed to be buried, the two surviving friends went to see him. As they stood looking down into the casket, one of them said, "Boy, don't he look natural. It looks just like him!"

The other one said, "Well, it ought to. It's him, ain't it?"

As they stood there with tears in their eyes, one said, "By golly, just for ol'time's sake we ought to have another drink with him. Let's just pick up ol' Joe and take him around to the corner bar." There wasn't anybody around, so they picked up Joe and headed for the pub. They took him to a dark, back corner, and propped him up on the barstool, fixing his arm so he wouldn't fall.

They sat there and drank several toasts and talked about the good times until one of them got hot and said, "Boy, it's kinda close in here. I think I'll step outside for a breath of air."

The other one said, "Well, you ain't leaving me in here by myself with Joe! I'm coming, too." And they stepped outside.

As soon as they left, the bartender came over, took one look at old Joe sitting there, and said, "Buddy, you look like the dickens. You've had enough. Let's go!"

Well, of course, Joe didn't move or say a word, which was not unusual since he was dead. So the bartender said again, "Okay, bud, you've had enough. Now, let's go outside. Come on!" He jiggled Joe's arm, which unpropped him, and Joe fell off the stool onto the barroom floor.

The bartender panicked and knelt down and tried to rouse his customer. When Joe didn't move, the bartender put his ear down to listen to his heart.

About that time, the two drinking buddies came back in, saw what was happening and said, "Hey, hold on here, bartender! What are you doing? Have you killed our buddy?"

The bartender jumped up off the floor and without hesitation blurted out, "The son-of-a-gun drew a knife on me!"

It's a Miracle! No, It's Not!

LONDON (AP)—A Roman Catholic doctor visiting the Vatican caused a few gasps when he climbed out of a wheelchair after being blessed by Pope John Paul II, but he says it was all a misunderstanding.

"I heard someone say, 'It must be a miracle,' but it wasn't—only an embarrassment," said Dr. Jan Lavric, an able-bodied general practitioner from Yorkshire in northern England.

Lavric said Wednesday he went to Rome with a group of disabled people last month. After he sat down in the wheelchair, the only seat left in the Vatican's audience chamber, a Swiss guard unexpectedly began wheeling him forward.

"I tried to stop him, but he told me, 'Don't exert yourself.' What would you do? I couldn't jump up and run away, that would have made things worse," he said.

After he kissed the Pope's hand and was wheeled away by the guard, he stood up and folded the chair and carried it off. Lavric said, "I must say they were all very surprised."

"Devil" Advocated Church Attendance

ERWIN (AP)—The devil picketed Porter's Chapel Church here Sunday, startling sinners, frightening small children, and exhorting passersby to stay away from church.

Folks who passed the little cinder block church on N.C. 82 saw a red-suited creature with forked tail plodding up and down in front of the church. He carried a pitchfork in one hand and a sign in the other that urged people not to attend services.

"People were frightened to death," said a deputy who asked not to be identified. "Little kids were crying and even some of the grown folks I saw didn't look any too comfortable. As for me, I thought it was pretty odd."

It turned out that the "devil" was only a Christian in disguise.

The Rev. Floyd S. Turlington, pastor of the church, told Harnett County deputies that he engineered the masquerade as an experiment in reverse psychology.

"If you tell people not to do something, then they're going to do it," he said. So Turlington, his assistant pastor, and a Sunday school teacher took turns playing the devil.

What Turlington had not counted on was the panic that resulted. Switchboards at the sheriff's office and the Erwin Police Department flashed with frantic calls.

North Carolina law prohibits persons over 16 from wearing masks in public places. Deputies said that since the masked man was on church property, they decided not to arrest him.

Turlington said that one passing motorist stopped his car and said, "I just want to shake the devil's hand. I'VE BEEN MARRIED TO HIS SISTER FOR A LONG TIME."

By Any Other Name

WASHINGTON, D.C. Richard V. Fitzgerald, chief counsel for the Office of the Comptroller of the Currency, uses self-directed humor in the form of a story about the legal profession:

. . . I am a lawyer, and like most of my colleagues suffer from the reputation of looking at almost any question narrowly. After all, that is what lawyers are trained to do.

When I was in law school at Maryland, one of my professors began his class every semester with a story about a judge intended to enlighten the students as to the nature of their calling:

A couple from an out-of-the-way rural area on the eastern shore—Sam Brown and Eliza Wells—were celebrating the fourth birthday of their son when they decided it was about time to get married.

They drove to the county seat, located the judge, and asked him to marry them. They knew nothing about the need for a marriage license, so the judge sent them to a county clerk in another office of the courthouse to get a license.

In due course they came back with a license, authorizing the judge to marry them. After inspecting it, the judge turned to Sam and said, "Sam Brown, is your name Samuel?"

"Yes, that's right," the man replied.

"Well," said the judge, "you have to go back and get your full name stated on a new license."

When the couple returned about an hour later, the judge inquired of Eliza if her full name shouldn't be Elizabeth.

"Yes, your honor, it is," she replied.

"Well," said the judge, "you have to go back and have your full name stated on a new license."

About an hour later, the couple again returned. After examining the license closely, the judge said, "Your license is in order now, and I have no choice but to marry you. But I want you to understand clearly, that boy of yours will remain a technical bastard."

Sam cleared his throat and said, "Well, judge, that ain't so bad. That's what the clerk said you are, but it hasn't stopped you from rising in life."

(Robert O. Skovgard's THE EXECUTIVE SPEAKER)

Quarterback Philosophy

One columnist tells about the sportswriter visiting the pro football Raiders' headquarters in California. He had just come from the Jack London historic monument and was still impressed.

During his interview with the team's quarterback, Ken Stabler, the writer quoted a sample of London's prose to him: "I would rather be ashes than dust. I would rather that my spark should burn out in a brilliant blaze than it should be stifled by dry rot. The proper function of men is to live, not exist." Stabler nodded his head.

"What does that mean to you?" the sportswriter asked.

"Throw deep," Stabler replied.

Lasting Love

Comment at the First Annual Friends of Fratello Foundation Lunch in Atlanta: North Carolina State coach Jim Valvano on roastee Mike Fratello, coach of the Hawks: "Fifty wins last year. He's the best. What will happen next year if he wins 28? Will you love him? Yeah . . . and you'll miss him, too."

The Count Down

A University of Alabama student was walking down the main street of Birmingham when he noticed a fellow wearing an Auburn jacket jumping up and down on a manhole cover in the middle of the street. As he jumped he was shouting: "Sixteen! Sixteen! Sixteen!"

Being from the University of Alabama he had seen a lot of loony things in his day, but this time curiosity got the better of him. He went over to the jumper and asked what was going on.

"Well," the man drawled, sounding like many a good ol' boy, "I'm hopping up and down on this manhole cover, as y'all can see." And he continued jumping up and down. Sixteen! Sixteen! Sixteen!"

"Oh, an Auburn fan, huh? I should have known." And with that, the Alabama student started to walk away.

"Hold on," the Auburn man shouted." "You ought to try it before you judge me so quickly."

"Don't be ridiculous," the man shouted back. "Why should I make a fool of myself jumping up and down on a manhole cover just because a goofy Auburn guy tells me I should?"

"Well," the Auburn man persisted, still hopping, "you're going to wonder all your days what enjoyment that Auburn fella got from this if you don't try it!"

No Alabama fan wants an Auburn fan to have something he doesn't have, so after a moment's thought, he turned back toward the Auburn man who was still happily hopping up and down and repeating, "Sixteen! Sixteen!"

"Okay," the Alabama student told him. "I'll try it." And he started hopping gingerly on the manhole cover.

"No, the Auburn man shouted. "You have to jump higher!" And the man jumped higher. "And, you have to yell, "Sixteen!" And the Alabama student jumped still higher and yelled, "Sixteen!"

When he made one particularly high jump the Auburn man suddenly moved the manhole cover and the guy fell through. The Auburn man put the cover back over the hold and began jumping up and down again. "Seventeen! Seventeen!!"

(Note: Auburn fans will notice the significance of the choice of numbers in the preceding joke.)

Fighting Flies

After a spat one morning, a young couple stormed around the house, ignoring each other, slamming doors, banging pots, and huffing until the lady had a problem with the long zipper in the back of her dress.

She backed up to her fuming hubby and silently pointed over her shoulder to her zipper, indicating that if he were any kind of husband at all, he would zip it up for her.

He grabbed the zipper tab, and with a quick slide pulled it to the top. Then—as they used to say—the devil flew in him and he couldn't resist. Up and down the zipper went, zip-zip-zip, as the hubby let all of his anger out.

Then the zipper broke, leaving the lady standing in her favorite dress with a broken zipper, mad as a wet hen at her husband, and late for work. The final straw came when hubby had to cut her out of the now worthless dress.

She thought about it all day, plotting revenge against the creep she loved. The more she thought, the madder she got.

Her chance for revenge came that night as she came home from work. There, sticking out from under the family car, was a pair of legs wearing pants. Grunts and sounds of heavy mechanical work came from the greasy darkness underneath.

The lady tried, but she couldn't resist. This was her chance.

She leaned over, grasped the pants zipper in her hand, and zipped up and down like crazy—a blur of motion until her anger abated.

Feeling smug, she walked in the house and headed for the kitchen.

There, sitting at the kitchen table, was her husband.

She stammered for a moment, felt faint, and sat down. She sat quietly for a few seconds, and then in a tiny voice and not really wanting to hear the answer, asked, "Who is that under the car?"

"That's Bill. He came to help me fix the muffler," her husband replied. Then she told him what had happened.

He, at least, thought it was funny, and the couple decided the only decent thing to do would be to explain to Bill why a neighbor lady was playing with his fly. They went back outside to where Bill's legs still protruded from under the car.

"Bill?" called the husband.

Silence.

"Bill?" the lady called nervously.

Still nothing.

The couple grabbed Bill's legs and pulled him out.

Bill was lying there, knocked cold as a cucumber with a nasty gash on his forehead from banging his head when a strange hand had fumbled with his fly.

Bill recovered nicely. He thought it was funny . . . once the swelling went down.

It's Your Turn to Work Magic

Why not start your own collection of humor cues now? It is a simple procedure, and this Genie knows that it does make a difference. First, make a list of all the personal humorous stories which involve you and your family, friends or acquaintances. Next, read several joke books and select only the jokes that make you burst out laughing. Then, as you hear or read stories or lines that really tickle your fancy, make note of them or clip them from reading material and drop in your cue file for future humor breaks.

Humor cues may be likened to good poetry or good music . . . the kind you love to hear again and again . . . . the type that never ages . . . the music that makes you want to get up and dance. Make them a part of your life.

Taking a humor break each day with your humor cues is an important step in developing a sense of humor. It may even result in a healthier, happier life. Regardless, taking daily humor breaks will definitely be invaluable in magically creating a humor-oriented lifestyle.